Theodore I
that

MW00877635

By Nicky Thomas

Table of Contents

Theodore Roosevelt: author, statesman, war hero, explorer, and the 26th President of the United States. This was a man that was able to pack a lot into his life and it is easy to see why he is considered to have been one of the most influential individuals to have ever been in charge of the U.S.

He is remembered for a number of major contributions in the United States. Through an effective foreign policy, he shaped the world in general. He may have come into his position of power through a stroke of luck on his part, but it was an opportunity that he grabbed and took control of during his eight years as a President.

However, it is also useful for us to not only look at the man who was President, but also how his life and career were shaped up until that point. After all, millions of people grow up with the dream of becoming the President, but very, very few ever achieve that.

We will see how this was an individual that was not afraid to stand up for what he believed in. He was a strong individual who never backed down from a fight even when the odds were so strongly stacked against him that he knew he was fighting a losing battle. He was a man of his word, a man who took the moral stance at any given opportunity. He was never afraid to step on the toes of those that deemed themselves to be bigger than, not only him, but the government in general.

Theodore Roosevelt went from an affluent background to one that made him the most powerful individual in the world, by leading a country that was becoming the dominant force in many spheres of life. He took the country into a new century and changed it for the better in ways that could never have been imagined previously.

So, what made him different? What made him stand out from the crowd? Why exactly is he still viewed with such affection more than a century after his Presidency ended?

Let us explore the man behind the Presidency.

Chapter 1: His Birth and Early Life

Theodore Roosevelt was born in New York City on October, 27th 1858. He was born at 28 East 20th Street and was the second of four children born to Theodore and Martha Bulloch Roosevelt. His family were related to the Dutch that had moved into the area in the 17th century. According to a variety of sources, his birth was easy for his mother.[1] At this point, it would have been easy to assume that this child would be nothing too special and would go on to take up an active role in the family and their way of life. Considering the period we are talking about, Roosevelt was born into a relatively wealthy family, thanks to his father being a successful businessman that imported glass as well as a burgeoning philanthropist. Indeed, his father was one of the most well-known philanthropists

---

[1]   . His birth is described in some detail by Morris.

in that part of the country. His mother, on the other hand, was originally from Georgia, where she had grown up on a plantation. It is said that she often struggled with having moved so far north, but effectively stuck it out for the sake of her marriage and family.

By all accounts, the father of Roosevelt was a strong character and it has previously been stated that he was the only individual that Roosevelt actually feared in his life. His father was viewed as being an energetic individual as well as a dominant figure, so it is easy to see how he could have played a major role in the life of Roosevelt. However, when he stated that he was afraid of his father, we are not sure as to what exactly he meant by that phrase. His father was a domineering personality, although we will see, when we work through his story, this was a personality that would develop in the younger Roosevelt as well, although it would be used in a far more productive way.

Roosevelt had an older sister called Anna. He was then followed by a younger brother by the name of Elliot and finally a younger sister called Corinne. However, we know little about his interaction with his siblings, as most of the stories about the young Roosevelt are, of course, focused primarily on him as an individual. There are no indications that he had anything other than a warm relationship with them.

From an early age, Roosevelt was affectionately known by the nickname of 'Teedie'; not a million miles away from the name he would become known by later on in life. Even though he was born into what many saw as being the perfect family, the young Roosevelt often suffered from illness that, at times, was near to being fatal. In particular, Roosevelt had issues with asthma, and this affected the way in which he was able to interact with others. It was also the reason why Roosevelt was actually educated at home, rather than mixing with other children, as it was felt that it was too dangerous for his health to be surrounded by too many different people.

As a child, it is known that he enjoyed taking part in intellectual activities, perhaps because it was rather difficult for him to have a love of more strenuous activities, due to his asthma. He is known to have had a love of books and would spend a considerable amount of time both studying nature via literature as well as getting into the great outdoors in order to take in what was around him. This was something that would go on to have an impact in his life later on, but that is one area that we will explore in more detail further on in the book.

Issues with the Civil War

The 1860's were a tough time in the U.S. thanks to the Civil War and it was particularly tough for the Roosevelt family. His father was pro-Union and worked on the side of President Lincoln due to a desire to improve the lives of both Union soldiers and their families. On the other hand, his mother, maternal grandmother, and aunt were all sending packages back to family that were behind enemy lines, as they were all Southern girls.

This led to some tension within the household, but for Roosevelt, it was also a rather exciting time. It is known that he loved the secrecy of effectively smuggling these support packages behind enemy lines. But at the same time, he held strong ideas of becoming a Union soldier and a war hero. It was a time of mixed messages, although the young Roosevelt would not develop into an individual who could be described as sending out mixed messages to people that he would go on to serve.

However, clearly the young Roosevelt was still of an age where he was unable to fully comprehend what was going on in the country, or the issues within his own family, leaving him relatively oblivious to many of the problems caused by the

Civil War. Overall, this part of his life would not go on to shape his ideas regarding war, which is rather surprising, considering that he would become quick to throw out the concept of the country using its military capabilities when he worked his way into a position of power.

Moving into the Teenage Years.

As the young Roosevelt moved into his teenage years what we see is a young man that took the advice of his father, who believed that the key to resolving his various health issues was physical exertion. This was something that appealed to Roosevelt. Indeed, this desire to improve his physical stature was actually something that would go on to save his life in more ways than one.

His father had long held the belief that this could be a way of helping his son deal with his asthma. It is known that on nights where Roosevelt was particularly suffering that his father would take him out for a ride in his carriage. The idea was that the wind in his face would effectively force air deep into his lungs, allowing him to breathe more easily.

In addition, his father also came to the conclusion that there might be something wrong with Roosevelt's eyesight when he noticed that Roosevelt was unable to see targets that other boys his age were able to shoot with some degree of accuracy. As a result, his father took him for an eye test, where it was discovered that Roosevelt was very near-sighted, leading to him being given glasses for the first time. This would, of course, go on to become virtually his trademark, but being able to see the world this clearly was something that would ultimately change the life of Roosevelt. Indeed, it opened up a brand new way of seeing things, and it is entirely possible that this discovery connected to his eyesight really did shape the rest of his life.

We previously stated how his father advised him to get more physical in order to combat his asthma and it led to a gymnasium being installed in the family home. It should be noted that the other children in the family also suffered from various physical ailments, so it was not purely for his own use. Roosevelt was then forced into taking part in a program of both gymnastics and weight-lifting to help him build his physique, since even his father stated, *"You have the mind but you have not the body. You must make the body."* Roosevelt took this advice to heart, leading to him developing what could only be described as a rugged physique. Furthermore, he also developed a love for boxing, wrestling, and horse riding, all activities that he would maintain an interest in throughout his life.

So, what can we say about the early childhood of Theodore Roosevelt? It was not unpleasant in any way and he also was not required to put up with various hardships that are often linked to other presidents. He came from a stable home where there were very few stresses to worry about and it was clear that he would be set up for life no matter what he decided to do as an adult. However, nobody would have predicted that they had a future President of the United States on their hands.

Chapter 2: His Education

We said in the first chapter how Roosevelt was educated at home due to his health issues, but this was the same for all of the children of the Roosevelt family. It is known that they had two tutors, their aunt, Anna Bulloch, as well as a French governess. Their mother also took an active role in their early education, but as they progressed and moved closer towards the idea of going to college, it is believed that she took more of a background role, and merely ensured that their children were indeed receiving the kind of tutoring that they required.

Considering he was educated purely at home, it was an achievement to then be admitted to the prestigious Harvard University in 1876. During his time there, he studied a range of subjects including zoology, German, natural history, composition, and also forensics. However, none of these subjects would go on to have any real role in his life apart from, perhaps, his desire to learn more about natural history, since an important aspect of his Presidency was the desire to protect natural resources across the United States.

We are still used to Harvard being regarded as a place of study for the elite and this was still the impression given by the university at the time Roosevelt attended. Indeed, it was seen by many as being nothing more than just a finishing school for the rich, to polish their skills prior to them entering either business, law, or politics. Going to Harvard would give you an advantage in life when you left there, but for Roosevelt it was more about the learning aspect.

Harvard University at that time was not seen in the most favorable light. Indeed, in 1876, Horace E. Scudder wrote an article in Scribner's Monthly where he voiced his rather dim opinion on what was going on within those hallowed corridors.

'That repression or even disdain of enthusiasm, that emulation of high-bred cynicism and arrogant coolness, which in a young man do not be-token the healthiest, strongest character, is prevalent. The diving fervor of enthusiasm is openly, or by implication, voted a vulgar thing."

This was the environment that the young Roosevelt would be launched into some three months after the article was published. However, from what we know about his time at Harvard, Roosevelt was doing what he could to battle back against the perceived stereotype of its students.

His various contemporaries were mainly at the top of society in and around Boston. However, as we have seen in the quote from Scudder, the way in which they behaved themselves or approached their studies was different from Roosevelt, although that is not to say that he was not influenced by those around him. In actual fact, it is accepted by various scholars that his ideas surrounding the concept of both class and even status in society were largely formed by his time at Harvard.[2]

Most of the students that were attending Harvard were aware of the fact that their future had mainly been mapped out for them already. This led to them simply not taking their studies as seriously as they should have, although the same could not be said for Roosevelt. For him, it was about furthering his education. But the same could not be said for most of his classmates. Instead, they saw this as a time to party. It is accepted that Roosevelt felt particular disdain for those students that saw fit to attend brothels and simply focus on socializing rather than improving themselves.

It is for that very reason that we see Roosevelt gravitating away from his fellow students and spending more time with his lecturers, with whom he felt that he would learn more.

---

[2] _ . Lansford P.11

A number of his classmates, who were later quoted regarding their experiences with the young Roosevelt, commented on the way in which he quickly became known for his enthusiasm and the vigor with which he would enter discussions and simply take hold of the entire situation. To many, his energy was limitless, a quality that would serve him well throughout his life, even though it was often seen as being quite antagonistic when he was younger.

However, in a sign that this was not the normal way of approaching discussions, it is rather interesting to note that a number of his classmates were reported to have found his approach as being rather disconcerting and offensive. Furthermore, various colleagues also regarded his enthusiasm in discussions or arguments are being a source of embarrassment, due to him simply being unable to control his passion.

To really show the way that a number of individuals felt about his approach, we can refer to an incident described by a contemporary of his time at Harvard, Bradley Gilman who observed Roosevelt having a discussion with two freshmen in the corridors.[3]

"I was struck by the earnestness with which he was setting forth some point to the other two. He emphasized his points by vigorous movements of the head, and by striking his right first into his left palm."

This is a powerful image. This was an individual that was forthright in his opinion and not afraid to speak his mind. It is perhaps no surprise for us to then discover that a number of fellow students at Harvard would go out of their way to avoid entering a discussion or debate with Roosevelt simply because of his overpowering nature.

---

[3] . Accounts of his time at Harvard have been chronicled by Harvard University.

Further evidence of his nature, and indeed his character, are even apparent in the way in which he would address individuals from some distance away. It was not regarded as being the done thing to shout across a courtyard in order to draw attention to yourself, but that was not something that appeared to be of concern to Roosevelt. The Rev. Sherrard Billings commented on how even his speed of movement was an issue at Harvard.

"When it was not considered good form to move at more than a walk, Roosevelt was always running."

We stated earlier how Harvard was regarded as being the last point whereby those from an elite background could socialize and tune the skills that would allow them to lead a prosperous life, but that was something that was of grave concern to Roosevelt. He had been taught that those from such a background should effectively go out of their way to give back to their community and to help those that were not as fortunate. This was something that stuck with Roosevelt. It led to him feeling a certain degree of disgust at what he viewed as an abuse of their elite position by so many of his contemporaries.

The problem for Roosevelt was his inability to keep these opinions to himself, which led to a number of discussions and arguments with those classmates that he felt were taking advantage of their situation. It is also felt by many that his time at Harvard really formed the basis for the position he would adopt in his political career against those in America that held so much power thanks to their wealth.

Athletics at Harvard

However, his time at Harvard was not all disappointing to Roosevelt, as he excelled at both his studies as well as athletics.

He had already spent time working on his strength and fitness for a number of years prior to his arrival at Harvard, and he quickly discovered various sports clubs that allowed him to indulge in his various passions while not interfering with his studies. Ideally, he would have enjoyed playing either football or baseball for the university, but issues with his eyesight meant that this was impossible. Indeed, he failed to really participate in any organized sports, although he was able to continue with his workouts.

Furthermore, we know that he did spend a reasonable amount of time in the gym and participated in boxing on a number of occasions. However, the cold winter months would always lead to various issues with his asthma, forcing him to drastically reduce time spent working out.

It is also believed that his involvement in athletics allowed him to eventually get closer to at least some of his classmates. Indeed, he would go on to establish a number of important relationships with various individuals who would themselves go on to have distinguished careers.

Studies at Harvard

When it came to his studies, then there is no doubt that Roosevelt excelled at Harvard. Indeed, he is often quoted as having regularly challenged his professors on a variety of points, such was his confidence. This argumentative approach was something that would ultimately become a cornerstone of his approach to politics, although that would be in a slightly more refined manner than the methods he employed during his time at Harvard.

To some, his penchant for tackling his professors stemmed from his previous education having come from personal tutors. He was used to being able to challenge them, and he simply took that approach with him to Harvard, even though it was different to how the majority of people saw their classes at the university. His professors themselves would have been taken aback by this approach as he was rather forceful in his demands that they answer his concerns and questions.

As a student, he was not outstanding in every subject, by any means. However, he was hard-working and diligent, and there is no doubt that he did outperform a number of his contemporaries. Of course, he would then go on to surpass them all with what he was able to achieve later on in life.

It is believed that Roosevelt long wished to become a scientist, but unfortunately for him, one of his poorest subjects was mathematics, and this led to him effectively being forced into a career in either politics or law. As it turned out, he would involve himself in both during his life.

That is not to say that he completely gave up on his love of science. Indeed, throughout his life, he would return to the wilderness and write books on subjects connected to nature. His love for it was apparent to all. However, he was unable to make any progress in this area during his time at Harvard, something that is known to have upset him a great deal.

By the time he was coming to the end of his time at Harvard, the young Roosevelt had to carefully consider the direction in which he wanted his life to go. After much thought, he came to the conclusion that working in law would have to suffice.

So what can we learn about the education of Roosevelt and how it shaped him as an adult? It shows us how his particular style of politics and tackling the issues of the day were influenced by his education. Having respect for those in positions of power did not mean he would not challenge them to explain their position, or point out that they were wrong.

Chapter 3: His Early Career

After graduating from Harvard, Roosevelt believed that his future lay in law and, as a result, he entered Columbia Law School. However, this was a part of his life that would not work out quite as he expected it to. It ended with him ultimately dropping out of college before he was able to graduate. It is important to point out that there were some pretty good reasons as to why he dropped out that we will cover later, but he was already becoming disillusioned with the concept of working in law prior to this happening.

For a number of reasons, this part of his life is something that is often quickly glossed over when in actual fact it tells us a number of things about not only him as a person, but also how he was always aware of what he should do with his life at any given time. It also shows how he was the type of individual who was quite happy to admit when they had made the wrong decision and then take steps to rectify things as quickly as possible.

It is fair to say that Roosevelt did not exactly set the world on fire during his time at law school, but he was still guilty of arguing his opinions at any given opportunity, which makes it rather bizarre that he did not fair well as a lawyer. It is strange to think that we know little about his ability to argue things from a legal perspective when you consider how good an orator he would become.

Those that have studied the life of Roosevelt have generally come to the conclusion that his decision to attend law school was not out of some absolute desire to become a lawyer. Instead, it is assumed that he came to the conclusion that he had to have some kind of profession and he was not too concerned about the law. He did not show the same kind of enthusiasm for his time at law school as he did either with his private tutors or at Harvard. There are various reasons why this may be the case.

The problem for him, if it can be judged as such, was that even Roosevelt himself understood that there was no actual need for him to go to another school as he didn't have to work in order to survive. For him, life was a bit easier than that, as even Roosevelt himself was quoted as saying:

"I had enough to get bread. What I had to do, if I wanted butter and jam, was to provide the butter and jam, but to count their cost as compared with other things. In other words, I made up my mind that, while I must earn money, I could afford to make earning money the secondary instead of the primary object of my career."[4]

---

[4] . Quote from Sharp p. 28.

It is obvious that Roosevelt was able to just relax if he wanted to do so, but the problem for him was that his family had a work ethic that did not allow this. To his family, he had to show that he was working on something.

The Roosevelt family had long felt the need to attempt to fulfill what they saw as their social responsibilities, as they came from a privileged background. They had to show that they were willing to help those in more need. This was also something that Roosevelt agreed with, so that may have been part of his reasoning as to why law was the avenue that he had decided to go down.

For some, the only appeal that there could have been for Roosevelt in law was that he could argue that the money was indeed of secondary importance. For him, understanding and then winning the cases would be seen as more important. Making a difference in the lives of the people he was representing allowed him to meet his social responsibilities at the same time. He never looked upon the industry as one that could make him fabulously wealthy.

Having his Eyes Opened to the Law

Roosevelt entered law school with some very set ideas as to what the law was like and how it helped people in need, but he rather quickly discovered that this was not exactly the case. Instead, he started to feel rather despondent that the big and powerful person in the case, no matter if it was plaintiff or defendant, would come out on top in more instances than not. At this point, he felt that the law was perhaps not as good as he thought.

This issue of things not being socially fair was something that would keep cropping up in his life and indeed, it would form a key part of his development as a politician. To Roosevelt, it was impossible for there to be a 'fair deal' which was a term that as we will see would go on to become

rather important for him during his time as
President.

Roosevelt and Thinking About Politics

It was during his time at law school that
Roosevelt began to really take more of an
interest in politics and attended some political
meetings. Considering the way in which he was
viewing the law, it is no surprise that he felt that
the only people that were able to tackle what he
saw as being social injustice were politicians. It
could be argued that it was at this moment that
he decided that a move from the law into the
world of politics would be best for him. It would
go on to become the best decision that he would
ever make in his life.

Throughout a relatively short period of time,
Roosevelt began to be drawn further into the
political world. In the process, it was becoming
more and more apparent to him that the appeal
of law was diminishing. He was becoming caught
up in the way in which politics were able to

influence various aspects of life, rather than him trying to specialize in one area. Roosevelt understood that politicians would work on the laws, the economy, conservation, civil rights, and so much more.

At the same time, his disillusionment with the law was also becoming far more apparent. He was of the opinion that it was just incapable of ruling in a fair manner. He had particular issues with the laws that dealt with the relationship between seller and consumer. In his opinion, the law should have made sure that both sides were able to benefit, but his understanding of the law led him to the belief that it would almost always side with the seller.

To Roosevelt, this was very wrong on a number of levels and he began to really feel that it was impossible for him to carry on in a profession that was going directly against his own personal beliefs and philosophy. The entire process was so taxing on his brain and morals that he felt compelled to leave the profession before he was really able to effectively begin. Indeed, for many, this was a clear early sign of how Roosevelt would always seek to take the moral stance.

Ultimately, Theodore Roosevelt decided to leave law school in 1881 and it was not as if he had a set plan in place, either. You must remember that he had already stated that earning money was a secondary thing and that it was more to do with finding a career that could make a difference to society and people in general. If working in the law was not the career for him, then it would not leave too many other options although it was becoming clear to Roosevelt that the world of politics might be better suited as his calling.

We said how he had started to attend political meetings during his time at law school. However, his idea of entering this notoriously tough world without having any kind of career to fall back on was different and showed that he was either extremely confident in his ability or that he was deciding to stick strongly to his principles of only doing something whereby he could help people.

However, his time as a politician would be covered in a series of highs and lows, with elections won and lost as well as missing out on key nominations due to his unique style and his refusal to back down from a fight.

So, how do we summarize his early career? Well, if we are being honest about it, then we have to come to the conclusion that he effectively did not have one, due to dropping out from law school early. It is difficult for us to come to any kind of a conclusion as to what his future might have been had he not gone to law school, as it was there that he began to feel the draw of politics and attended his first political meetings. How far he expected to go in the world of politics is up for debate.

Chapter 4: His Developing Family Life

Clearly the family life of Roosevelt was something that would develop throughout his lifetime, but we will deal with his personal life in the one chapter for ease of reading.

Theodore Roosevelt was a strong family man. This was something that is known about him even from his days as a child. He idolized his father and at the same time adored his mother and even after their respective deaths he made sure that he remained in close contact with his siblings throughout his life. To him, they formed an integral part of who he was and how he had been shaped as a child and this was something that he took with him when he began to look at creating his very own family.

The first moment in his life that we should mention was his very first marriage at the age of

22 to a leading socialite of the time, Alice Hathaway Lee. She was the daughter of a prominent banker. They had a daughter in 1884 by the name of Alice Lee Roosevelt. However, the joy would be very short-lived for the family, with the wife of Roosevelt dying just two days after the birth of their child, from what was described as a kidney problem.

This devastated Roosevelt, as now he was without a wife and yet had a very young child to bring up. This was not the only death that he had to deal with at that time; in a cruel twist of fate his beloved mother, Mittie, had died of typhoid fever in the exact same house only eleven hours earlier.

Due to this double hit, it is perhaps no surprise that he at first decided to leave his daughter in the custody of his sister while he went through the grieving process. However, he would assume custody of her once again by the time she was three years old. In the meantime, he took time in order to attempt to heal. He had been very close to his mother, and of course to his young wife; it would have been a difficult double blow for anybody to take. The very fact that he was able to not only come back from it, but do so in a spectacular way, tells you a lot about the character of the man.

It is clear that the death of Alice hit Roosevelt hard. Indeed, in his diary he is known to have just marked the date with an X and noted that the light had gone out of his life. He would hardly write about her throughout the rest of his life.

The grieving process was interrupted by Edith Kermit Carow. Edith would go on to not only become the love of his life, but his companion until his dying days.

Edith was hardly unknown to Roosevelt, as she had grown up beside him as a child. She was also the best friend of Roosevelt's younger sister,

Corinne. It is also generally accepted that she was the first individual outside of his immediate family that Roosevelt actually played with. The two would play in the same kindergarten as children. Indeed, it is also suggested that the mother of Roosevelt felt that there was some kind of friendship developing between the two, although clearly it was impossible to predict that things would develop to this extent later on in life.

Furthermore, it is believed by some that the two of them developed some kind of relationship as teens, so they were romantically involved to a certain extent, but this romance came to an end without anybody really being aware. However, it is believed that it was not long after the end of this romance that Roosevelt began to attempt to woo Alice Lee. Edith would be present at their wedding not long after he graduated from college.

However, after the untimely death of Alice in 1884, Edith once again became important in the life of Roosevelt, rekindling their relationship in 1885. The relationship is known to have started before it was announced to the public, as Roosevelt was of the opinion that, as he was still getting over the death of his first wife, that it would be too soon for him to reveal that he was in another relationship. They were ultimately married in London on December 2nd 1886.

The couple then embarked on a 15 week honeymoon tour of Europe, before returning to the United States to allow Roosevelt to continue with his career. Upon returning, the couple moved into the house on Long Island close to Oyster Bay that he had initially started to build for his first wife. However, he did change the name of the home from LeeHolm to Sagamore Hill. This home would ultimately become their favorite place to retreat to, even when Roosevelt was in the White House. After his death it would also become the place where Edith would remain for the rest of her living days.

After his marriage to Edith, he sought to regain custody of his daughter from his first marriage. He felt that they were now a strong enough family, and he had recovered from his initial loss sufficiently, to provide her with the upbringing that she deserved. Edith and himself would go on to have a total of five children with four sons and one daughter, with Edith also having at least one miscarriage that we are aware of.

The interesting thing about this family is that the American people really took to them, especially during the years in the White House. They were the first example of America falling in love with the First Family, something that has carried on since then. Indeed, the media of the time would often report and comment on issues regarding the family, so you can see how it is perhaps a precursor to what has gone on since.

It is no surprise that there are a number of photographs of the family at the White House, as they were major celebrities at a time where the concept of the celebrity did not quite exist in the way we are familiar with today.

Moving Around the Country

Even though the Roosevelts did have their home on Long Island to go back to, life as a politician involved moving around a number of times. This was the case with Theodore Roosevelt, but his wife and children were only too happy to follow suit in order to support him and also keep the family unit together.

However, by the time Roosevelt became President and moved into the White House, the family had already lived in Washington D.C. on two different occasions. They initially lived in the Washington area between 1889 and 1895, when Roosevelt worked as the chairman for the United States Civil Service Commission. They were then forced into moving back to Washington just two years later, in 1897 until 1898, when Roosevelt was the assistant secretary for the navy. This delighted his wife and was extremely important for Roosevelt.

Aside from living in Washington, they also had to move back closer to their roots in 1899, when Roosevelt became the governor of New York. However, this would only last for another two years, before the family was forced into moving back to Washington D.C for a third time (although this was to live in the White House, which was a completely different proposition for them.)

As a rather interesting aside, presidents since Roosevelt can thank his wife for their having more space in the White House. It was accepted by those that had come before him that things were slightly cramped in the building and that it was not actually that suitable for the first family to live in. However, when the Roosevelt family moved in, they had a number of children to contend with, as well as various staff and security, and it was just not possible for them to live there as it was.

As a result, Edith Roosevelt set about changing things in the White House. She was the main instigator behind the construction of the West Wing, which would be used to house all of the different Presidential offices. Up until this point, these offices were crammed in beside the living area for the family, which was hardly an ideal solution. Indeed, it should also be noted that even though it was often referred to as the White House, that did not become its official name until Theodore Roosevelt made it so.

His Relationship with His Family

There is no doubt that Roosevelt loved being the President, but he was actually prouder of being a father and took great delight in seeing his children grow and develop throughout their lives. This feeling towards his family was something that was readily apparent and it contributed to the way in which they were viewed in society.

Indeed, we can actually get a glimpse into the way in which he viewed his family in a letter that he wrote to his 15 year old son, Kermit upon his re-election in 1904.

"No matter how things came out, the really important thing was the lovely life with Mother and you children, and that compared to this home life everything else was of small importance from the standpoint of happiness." [5]

As we can see from this quote, it is clear that he was quite content to put family before anything else, even a position as powerful as President, and this idea can be stressed even further by another quote:

---

[5] _The quote itself is taken from The Theodore Roosevelt Association website.

'There is no form of happiness on the Earth, no form of any success of any kind, that in any way approaches the happiness of the husband and the wife who are married lovers, and the father and mother of plenty of healthy children.'[6]

The problem for Roosevelt was that there were a number of times during the early lives of his children that he was forced to be away from them. This was troubling to him, as he struggled with being away from those he loved the most. Ultimately, it would lead to Roosevelt writing them a series of letters, in order to show that they were still utmost in his thoughts. These letters would then form a book, *Theodore Roosevelt's Letters to his Children*, that was published around the time of his death and became a huge hit. Indeed, this book only further cemented the reputation and feelings of appreciation towards the family that had been with them during their time in the White House.

---

[6] Quote from the Theodore Roosevelt Association.

His family was capable of affecting him in ways that nothing else could. Indeed, he was quick to announce when he was proud of their achievements in life, and it is also known that the death of his son in World War I sent him spinning into a deep depression from which he never really recovered to any great extent. Aside from that one issue, his family life was happy, and he was more than content to get away from the world of politics and spend time with those he loved the most.

Chapter 5: His Introduction into Politics

When it comes to his introduction to politics, we have to go back slightly in time to when he was a student at Harvard, as the roots of a number of his beliefs were more than likely shaped during this period of his life.

During his first few years at the university, Roosevelt's father had become more interested in, not only politics, but the concept of political reform. He is known to have taken quite a firm stance against what he saw as the Republican machine in and around New York State, and he made some in-roads in his early political career. Indeed, such was his success as an advocate for political reform, that it led to President Hayes electing Roosevelt Senior to the position of federal tariff collector for New York.

This was a position that held some prominence, but he was not finished there with his potential political career. The move by Hayes to appoint Roosevelt senior to this position was a clear attempt at trying to fight back against those he saw as having too much political power. He was aware that Roosevelt senior would not stand for insolence and corruption.

However, there was a problem. There were enough individuals in the Republican party, including Senator Roscoe Conkling, that when the appointment of Roosevelt senior was put to Congress, the move was defeated 31 votes to 25.

This is the moment regarded by many as being a key point in the political ideas of Roosevelt. To him, the fact that a handful of powerful individuals was able to block reforms that he saw as being essential was indicative of how corrupt politics were, especially within the Republican Party. This unsettled him to such an extent that he there and then decided that something would have to happen to the way in which businesses and certain key individuals were able to work against justice. To Roosevelt, it was clear that the welfare of the people in general was the most important thing, and anything that got in the way had to be dealt with accordingly. It was an issue that he would deal with time and time again by the time he got to the White House.

It is difficult to state that if his father had been treated better then perhaps Roosevelt would have mellowed slightly in his approach to the issue of corruption. However, that was not the case, and Roosevelt would make an entire career out of the concept of taking those individuals and companies to task for their illegal and unfair methods of doing things.

Getting Started in Politics

In order to chart the political development of Roosevelt, we have to go back to 1882 and his election to the New York State Assembly, as this was the first time he made it publicly known that he was interested in developing a career in politics. By this time, Roosevelt had already shaped a number of his key ideas. His desire to get into local politics was being driven by his desire to right what he saw as a number of wrongs, and even a number of crimes, against not only the country but the general public.

At this point in history, the entire local political scene was not for the faint-hearted. It was a tough place to operate, with so many individuals desperate to further their own cause, or being open to corruption, that it was difficult for an individual to really strike out on their own. This was especially true in and around New York, where things were tougher than in most places. Roosevelt was not put off by this prospect and instead threw himself into it from the outset.

However, the one problem that Roosevelt faced was that he was largely restricted in the political party that he could really follow. He was regarded as being an aristocrat and for a number of people there was the opinion that the Democrats were slightly rougher and tougher in their approach to life. This was then seen as not being a good fit for his upbringing although it could be argued that a number of his policies and political beliefs were aligned more towards the Democrats. It put him in a pretty unique position although Roosevelt made it clear that he was his own man and would not be influenced by what he was expected to do by others.

It was not all plain sailing for Roosevelt, as he made it clear that he intended to become involved in the world of politics, and it was his own friends that were the most critical of his ideas. However, it should be noted that most of his friends were either lawyers or working in senior positions in banking, and to them the idea of being a politician was something that was just not good enough. In other words, there was a touch of snobbery about their approach to life and as a result they were guilty of scoffing at the ideas held by Roosevelt.

This opinion was then only capable of reinforcing ideas that Roosevelt already had regarding the influence that business and the world of finance had on politics. His friends were of the belief that they were able to use their influence from their own particular world in order to effectively make political change. This was something that had upset Roosevelt for some time, as he had already noticed how business and powerful individuals had managed to have a negative impact on the potential future career of his own father.

Developing his Career as a Politician

Even though his friends were clearly against his idea of becoming a politician, it was not something that he would allow to unduly influence him. Instead, Roosevelt's ideas on how to progress as a politician were rather distinct, as he understood that it was important for him to stay close to those that were regarded as being influential on the smaller, local level. This in itself was a clever approach to take, considering what was at stake, and this ability to identify the correct people to target was something that he would continue to take advantage of throughout his career.

To some, it may have appeared to have been a waste of time dealing with people that were so far down the political ladder, but for Roosevelt it was all about getting himself noticed. He understood that he had to begin his political career at the local level, and yet there was so much competition that he also understood that it would be difficult to get noticed, considering he was in his early 20's. Indeed, he would be up against other individuals with a considerable amount of experience, so he had to be clever to get his foot in the political door.

His plan was to work his way into the position whereby, whenever an opportunity arose, they would feel compelled to turn to him rather than anybody else, simply because he was always on their mind. Ultimately, it would prove to be a wonderful plan that would eventually pay dividends, although it would prove to be a rather long road for him to travel.

His plan actually worked better than perhaps even he could imagine. Soon after beginning to attend Republican meetings on a regular basis, Roosevelt would find himself with two important friends, Joe Murray and Jake Hess. Murray was regarded as a rising star, whereas Hess was the local boss, and they both took a liking to Roosevelt. Indeed, Murray would refer to Roosevelt as being his protege, although both understood that Roosevelt was more than likely going to turn into a real star in the Republican movement. It would, therefore, be in their interest to try to get him on their side, as they clearly saw that politics was largely about self-preservation, at least when it came to your own career.

The problem for the two of them, and for Roosevelt, was that they became involved in their very own power struggle. By the end of it all, the one person that came out of the struggle in a more powerful position was neither Murray or Hess, but Roosevelt.

This is actually a prime example of the power of the man and the way in which he was able to take a situation and turn it around to his advantage. He was able to identify a potential weakness that he could then exploit, although nobody would have expected him to run with this opportunity quite as much as he did.

The Street Cleaning Incident

An early lesson that Roosevelt had managed to learn was that a politician could make wonderful inroads even when they were fighting what was effectively a lost cause as long as they put across their side of the argument and stuck to their guns. This is the exact method that he employed in what could be referred to as "the street cleaning incident", which took place during the power struggle between Murray and Hess.

There had been a debate regarding street cleaning and the use of the "machine", and Roosevelt had made it clear that he backed a more nonpartisan approach to the issue. Both Murray and Hess were aware that Roosevelt would not be in a position to win a vote on the issue, and indeed this was the case, with him being almost routed in the process. However, the actual vote itself was not the reason why Roosevelt took this approach. Instead, it was his way of showing that he would not back down when he believed in something, even when the odds were stacked against him. He may have lost the vote, but he won a lot of admirers for his steadfast approach and the way he felt strongly enough to fight a losing battle until the end.

It may have been a relatively small issue to contend with, but it gave a glimpse into the future as Roosevelt would go on to show that he was never afraid to tackle problems that many before him had felt unable to contend with. The odds being stacked against him would only lead to him fighting harder for the cause, particularly if it was something that he completely believed in.

1881 – Getting into Politics

The year 1881 was undoubtedly a key year in the development of the political career of Theodore Roosevelt, and set him on the path to the White House.

This year was one that would involve elections. The Republican Party was actively looking for a candidate that they could put up for the New York Assembly. At first, Roosevelt was not interested in potentially running for this position and indeed we are not even aware of whether or not he realized that there was a potential opening. However, Murray was well aware, and both himself and the Republican leaders in New York all agreed that Roosevelt was something special.

As a result, he was encouraged to run for office and would receive the full backing of the party. It may have been a lowly position in the world of politics, but for Roosevelt it would provide him with some much needed experience, something he was seriously lacking in. It was an opportunity that he would ultimately take, even if it did require some prompting on the part of others.

Being given the nomination was something that came as a surprise to Roosevelt. He is quoted as saying so when asked about his move into politics.

"I had at that time neither the reputation nor the ability to have won the nomination for

myself, and indeed would have never thought to try for it."[7]

In other words, Roosevelt was appearing to suffer from a lack of self-confidence at this moment and we have to consider that history would have been very different had Murray not gone out of his way to convince him that this position would be perfect for him. Considering that he was only too willing to becoming embroiled in discussions, it is rather peculiar to then discover that he had second thoughts about moving into politics when presented with this opportunity.

Roosevelt would go on to win the position, serving in the assembly for three years. This was a time where the young Roosevelt had to contend with a steep learning curve. We know that he had his eyes opened to more corruption and the way

---

[7] _ Quote from Andrews P.62

in which certain spheres of society had too much say in the political world.

By the end of this period, Roosevelt had come to the conclusion that corruption was rife throughout the state, and from that he could make an educated guess that it would be a similar picture elsewhere across the country. This appalled him, and he would go on to make beating corruption an absolute cornerstone of his political career. However, at this stage, he was still blind to understanding just how big the problem was and how corruption covered almost every aspect of society.

Those three years were a torrid time for him, but Roosevelt himself felt that it was able to provide him with a strong foundation to build upon throughout his political career. Indeed, it actually helped to strengthen his convictions that he had to tackle certain key issues, with them forming the basis of his domestic policies.

To show the scale of the problem in the eyes of Roosevelt, we should mention that he was of the belief that as much as one in three members of the legislature were corrupt in some way, which is a staggering amount. However, all that this meant to him was that he had to be prepared to tackle corruption on two different fronts, both within the legislature itself, as well as with those individuals and businesses from outside that wished to wield undue influence. It would not be an easy task, but it was one that he wished to tackle anyway.

Throughout his time in the New York Assembly, Roosevelt fought hard to introduce a number of changes that he strongly believed would be beneficial to the overall health of society in and around the city. However, each step of the way, he had to deal with corruption from every conceivable angle, and it is crazy to think how this was the case, even when he was battling to open up a new park in the city. The arguments against this would pale into insignificance compared to when he pushed forward a bill whereby various businesses would be required to pay higher taxes while every day New Yorkers would have their tax bill cut.

We said how this was a learning curve for Roosevelt and when we get to the end of his three year term, what we have is an individual that has a much better understanding of the strong link between business and politics. This was something that sat rather uncomfortably on his shoulders and indeed as we will see it was a link that he would work hard at removing as he moved up higher on the political ladder.

A Glimpse at the Future

We must jump back slightly in time to before his election in order to get a glimpse into the future of Roosevelt and the way in which he would handle various situations.

It was accepted by the Republican Party that Roosevelt was rather wet behind the ears in the political sense and indeed that was one reason why Hess was initially against his nomination. However, after it was agreed that Roosevelt would be put forward, everybody pulled together in order to provide him with the best possible campaigning platform.

The only problem for those involved was that they had not counted on Roosevelt being so forthright with his opinions, although they would encounter them on the campaign trail. However, this in itself should have perhaps come as no surprise, as Roosevelt was no shrinking violet when it came to letting people know his opinions on those issues that he felt most strongly about.

When it came to campaigning, it was believed at the time that you should try to talk to saloon keepers. However, it was also well known that those same saloon keepers were guilty of dealing with bribes between not only politicians but also local government officials and the police. This was clearly going to be something that Roosevelt was going to be against, as it was more than just a pet hate of his. The only problem was that neither Hess nor Murray could predict what would happen as soon as he went on the campaign trail with them after his nomination.

It is known that the three of them embarked on the campaign trail and were planning on paying particular attention to taverns, although this approach began to crumble upon entering the first tavern owned by an individual by the name of Valentine Young.

What then occurred was clearly a misunderstanding on how both sides would work if Roosevelt was elected. In his mind, he would be in a position whereby he would be able to help the tavern owner with various issues. However, Mr Young held the opinion that he would be the one that would ultimately be telling the young politician what to do. Clearly, Roosevelt was never going to be the kind of individual that would take kindly to a tavern owner telling him what to do. The two of them clashed, not only with the stance that they believed Roosevelt should take, but also because they would both refuse to back down.

This point was further stressed because Young was of the opinion that fees for taverns were too high and that Roosevelt should then lower them, merely because he suggested it and had complained that they were unfair. Roosevelt, on the other hand, held a completely different opinion. To him, the fees were actually too low compared to other businesses, and he always held the belief that he had to seek a fair deal for everybody, no matter their industry or reasons behind certain beliefs. He felt that the fees had to be increased, which was a point of view that would not go down well with Mr Young.

As a result, both Hess and Murray not only quickly ushered him out of the tavern, but they also ushered him into another street. They would then go back to the various taverns along Sixth Street and campaign for him while he got to work on a quieter street where they believed he would be able to do less damage to his chances of being elected.

Winning the Election and Moving to Albany

After considerable amounts of hard work, and even with Roosevelt being close to messing up his campaigning due to his outspoken ways, Roosevelt won the election and as a result he had to Albany in order to take up his seat in the assembly. He was the youngest state legislator to have ever won an election in New York and the Republican Party felt justified in their selection of him. Little did they understand that he would begin to make a name for himself pretty much from the beginning of his time in Albany.

This position was something that Roosevelt took on with some gusto and developed into his normal way of doing things. Indeed, by the time he reached the end of his three year term, he had set new records for the number of bills to have been introduced, even though he was the youngest by some considerable margin.

Indeed, to really show how seriously he was taking this position, we only have to look at the way in which he introduced four bills within the first 48 hours of taking up his seat. It is no surprise that he was often referred to as being akin to a whirlwind. These first four bills also give us an insight into the things that were most important to him and it shows us how his political point of view was shaped from an early age. The first four bills focused on the need for judicial reform, financial reform in New York, electoral reform, and also improving water purification. As you can begin to imagine, to suggest so many reforms within days of being approved to the Assembly led to him ruffling more than just a few feathers.

Hit and Miss with the Bills

Even though he got off to such a fast start, Roosevelt did learn a key lesson relatively early on in his political career, which was that it is not how many bills you present to the House, but the number that get approved that is important. Indeed, with his first four bills, only one of them was passed, as the Assembly approved a much adapted version of his electoral reform.

The fact that only one bill was passed was not of a major concern to Roosevelt, as he had other issues that he had to contend with. He had his heart set on dealing with the problem of corruption. When he decided to begin tackling this issue, he hardly started off at the bottom, as he had been informed of an extensive problem involving a number of prominent individuals within New York.

These individuals were actually other politicians, so it was striking home for Roosevelt, as he was left wondering exactly who around him was part of the corruption. In this instance, the corruption was focused on these politicians with the railroad magnate Jay Gould.

Thanks to the corruption that existed, politicians were willing to put through various pieces of legislation that were always going to be in favor of what Gould was wanting with the railroad. However, it was not as if the public of New York were unaware of what was going on. There are reports of how the public was annoyed at what was happening, but they were even more irritated at the fact that the Legislature was clearly not doing anything to tackle the problem.

For Roosevelt, this was not something that could be left alone, but he made the mistake of asking people in senior positions within the Republican Party what they intended to do about the problem of corruption. He was rather taken aback when he was not only told that they would do nothing about it, but that they wanted him to just ignore the issue as well. This put Roosevelt in a difficult situation as he was not the type of person that could just ignore it, leading to him stating that he would tackle the problem on his own.

Tackling Corruption

Roosevelt was either not aware of the size of the problem that he was trying to tackle, or else he was too stubborn to back down from a fight. The main focus of his attention was the Attorney General, Theodore Westbrook.

1882 saw Roosevelt making a speech in the Assembly that left people open-mouthed in astonishment. His speech focused on highlighting the issue of corruption and demanding that action be taken against the Attorney General. It is perhaps of no surprise that the Assembly was adamant that nothing would be done, although this was not going to be the end of the matter for Roosevelt, who vowed to continue his fight.

At the end of the day, Roosevelt was so persistent with his campaign that the media eventually caught wind of the problems in the Assembly. It was only after they made the issue known to the wider public that the Assembly were virtually shamed into launching an investigation. However, this was only a token gesture, because not only did the investigation not do much, there were no charges or changes brought about as a direct result. The Assembly thought they had done their part, although clearly Roosevelt was not content at the outcome, as nothing had been resolved.

It was not all bad for Roosevelt, because his desire to bring the Attorney General to account for his actions was lauded in the press, and it helped to further cement his reputation as somebody who was going to try to defend the people. The fact that he would always refuse to back down would help to put him in a good position in the future.

His Second Year in the Assembly

The people were of the opinion that Roosevelt had performed admirably in his first year in the Assembly, so it was relatively easy for him to be elected for a second year. However, expectations would be higher this time around, although he was confident enough that he would not disappoint them.

The fact that he had attempted to impeach the Attorney General did not seem to really hamper him too much, as the party sought to appoint him as a speaker in the Legislature. The only problem for him was that the Democrats held sway in the Assembly, with the outcome being that Roosevelt was elected as the speaker for the minority.

In his second year, he continued down the road of trying to introduce various reforms in much the same vein as his first year. He undoubtedly impressed during this second year, but his third year in the Assembly was not quite what he expected. The people seemed to be on his side, but the people in his own party did not have the same opinion. They felt that Roosevelt was actually causing too many problems and being a nuisance. They felt that he was too reckless for them to fully support him, unless he changed his ways.

In his third year he had one major issue that he wished to address, altering the way in which the Aldermen of New York City had a say in the local politics. To Roosevelt, the main problem was that they were heavily involved in the appointment of the mayor, and in his opinion that was something that the everyday citizen of New York should also be involved in.

Furthermore, he was also invited to partake in a committee that was established to tackle the problems with the labor force, as well as the health of those individuals that worked in the burgeoning cigar industry. As part of his job, he was invited to tour an actual factory. This is regarded as being the moment where Roosevelt began to feel the need to look at tackling the way in which the workforce was being treated, as well as the kind of conditions they were working in.

Upon the arrival at the cigar factory, Roosevelt was taken aback by what he saw. The factory amounted to a working slum. He would encounter two families both working and living in just two rooms and all for the sum of $1 a day. Roosevelt was horrified and he became aware of the fact that these workers were having to exist in horrible conditions. Indeed, he even remarked to others that he was completely unaware that people in New York were being forced into existing in these kinds of conditions, and that there was no other option but to try to force through changes to bills that were designed to drastically improve those conditions.

The Next Step up the Ladder – The Cities Committee

He was appointed to a role in the Cities Committee. This was something that appealed to Roosevelt, as he was of the opinion that it would allow him to carry out much needed reforms. He believed that this would be the perfect opportunity to push forward certain ideas, as he had more power at his disposal and was likely to face less opposition. Clearly, he did not understand that there were still various people at different levels of the political ladder that would try their best to prevent him from making the changes that he would have liked to implement.

He looked at the session of the Legislature in 1884 as his chance to make these key changes, with it ultimately leading to him introducing a series of bills early on in the session linked to liquor laws. It is unknown how Mr. Young would have taken to this relatively young upstart going against his wishes, when those before him would have probably swung the other way. During this time, he sought to make more changes than any other legislator, although his changes were hit and miss.

It is at this point that we should also mention a trip taken by Roosevelt that, once again, helped to further shape the way in which his views developed. After the death of his mother and first wife, Roosevelt took a trip to Dakota where he spent time living the life of a cowboy and learning various tricks. However, this trip was about more than just trying to learn how to rope and survive in the American wilderness. Instead, it showed him just how important this part of American society was and that there was a need to preserve it as much as possible.

Furthermore, this life also taught him the importance of being an individual, and it inspired him enough to lead to him writing a book based on examining the West and the concept of the wilderness. It was a period of growth, and there is no doubt that it had an impact on his political beliefs, something that would have an influence on, not only Roosevelt, but eventually the entire country. Indeed, Roosevelt was of the opinion later on in life that there was no way that he would have ever been president had he not gone to Dakota at this point in his life.

1884 – The Presidential Election

As we move into 1884, we enter presidential elections, but Roosevelt himself was not standing for election. Instead, he made it clear who he was backing. In this instance, he vowed to support Senator Edwards of Vermont. The problem for him was that the GOP were determined to back Senator Arthur from New York State.

As was the norm for him, he never felt as if he could back down from a fight, and through persistent arguing he did manage to sway substantial support. In doing so, he managed to further his own reputation within the state of New York, something that would be of advantage to him in the near future.

Indeed, it could easily be argued that the way in which he conducted himself at this point helped to pave the way for his next step up the political ladder, a run at becoming the mayor of New York.

He had been absent from the political scene for two years and he felt revitalized and ready to tackle whatever this murky world was about to throw at him. His first step was to become the Republican candidate for the position of the mayor of New York, although even Roosevelt was of the opinion that he would be unable to win the election. However, he still felt that it was an important step to take, as it showed he was back in politics. His feeling that he would lose the election would ultimately turn out to be correct.

Roosevelt understood that there was no need for him to rush back into politics. Indeed, he was quite content to sit back and patiently wait for the correct opportunity to present itself, although that is not to say that he was not becoming involved in anything of note.

What then followed was a period of some three years where Roosevelt was not as active, until President Harrison opted to appoint him to one of the positions of the Civil Services Commission, a position that Roosevelt felt was perfect for him to introduce some of the reforms that were close to his heart.

The Civil Services Commission

Roosevelt was able to win this position as a direct result of his campaigning on behalf of Harrison in the 1888 election. Indeed, he was responsible for carrying out a number of speeches declaring the virtues of electing Harrison as President. After he was successful in his campaign, Harrison was of the opinion that Roosevelt should be rewarded for his efforts. Roosevelt had previously been an advocate for change and reform within the realm of the civil service, and yet he had been blocked when trying to make changes at lower levels. However, this was no longer going to be an issue for him, as he was being given new powers that were difficult to stop, a position that he would go on to relish.

Roosevelt approached this position from the basis of three simple principles that were all connected to his belief that he was going to have to revamp the civil service and improve the overall way in which it worked. He also believed that making changes would ultimately result in the government being able to attract a better quality candidate, and the country as a whole would then be more likely to prosper.

He looked at it in three ways. First, he held the opinion that every citizen should have an equal opportunity to develop a career in the civil service. Secondly, federal jobs should only ever be given to those that had merit and would be able to justify themselves in those positions. Finally, under no circumstances should the public find themselves in difficulty due to their political persuasion.

As the commissioner, he became focused on the need to tackle abuse and corruption within the government, as well as becoming a vocal opponent of the spoilsman. It was a position that he would hold until 1895 and during that time he was able to make a major impression on not only those involved in the commission, but across the country in general.

Very few people were actually happy at the prospect of Theodore Roosevelt being given this position. He had made it clear that he was not turning a blind eye to the corruption that surrounded him, nor was he going to just keep quiet about it. There may have been some changes made after the Pendleton Act, but the reality was that most things had stayed the same, with corruption continuing to be rife.

For those that were involved in this world, it must have been a painful experience to learn that Roosevelt had been appointed to the commission. The very last thing that they would have wanted was somebody who was an actual activist and who would be seeking to enforce the law at every given opportunity. A number of people must have looked at their future and felt that it was very bleak indeed.

Roosevelt had already encountered corruption in the Civil Service while he was working in the New York Assembly, and he understood that it was a major issue. However, he was also aware that only those in charge of the Civil Service were in a position to make the relevant changes. Now he was one of those people, and he had the desire to do whatever was required to push through those reforms.

Indeed, he made his views on issues such as the spoils system very clear indeed:

"No republic can permanently endure when its politics are corrupt and base. The spoils system, the application in politics of the degrading doctrine that to the victors belong the spoils, produces corruption and degradation...The spoils-monger and the spoils-seeker invariably breed the bribe-taker and the bribe-giver, the embezzler of public funds and the corrupter of voters."[8]

There can be no mistaking what Roosevelt was saying here. To him, so many aspects of politics appeared corrupt that the entire country was in danger. It was clear to him that he had a major job on his hands, but it was not a job that he would ever be able to shy away from.

---

[8] . Quote from Benge P.113

One of the problems that he initially faced in this position was the way in which the commissioners were actually viewed by the public. On most occasions, their jobs had been a result of the spoils system, so immediately it seemed to be a contradiction in what Roosevelt was campaigning against. In addition, they were lazy individuals that were completely ineffective at enforcing the law, simply because they appeared to be more content being paid while doing nothing rather than trying to make those all important changes.

As a result, Roosevelt came to the conclusion that he had no option but to seek to change the institution that he was now part of before he would be in a position to change society for the better. This was clearly going to be a major job.

His first task was to alter the examinations that any potential worker for the Civil Service had to take prior to being accepted into the position. They were too easy and not reflective of the job in question, although he also believed that actual experience should count for a lot more than the ability to answer questions or deal with theory.

He held the belief that it was better for the country if those individuals working for the Civil Service were able to perform certain practical tasks. After all, those working in the west would be better served if they were skilled horsemen or able to shoot straight, no matter how good their spelling was.

At the same time as his attempts to alter how the commission went about its business, Roosevelt was also determined to take the Pendleton Act and start to employ it on a regular basis. This in itself was going to shake up many aspects of society, since it had been largely ignored since it was brought into law.

In order to show that he was indeed serious about tackling various issues, Roosevelt made his way to his old stomping ground in New York

City. He was already aware of the level of corruption that existed on various levels in the city and he believed that if he was serious about trying to clear things up that he should do so in his own back yard first.

However, his first act was to actually investigate claims that there was corruption within the customs house in the city. What he found was that a number of people had been leaked a series of questions for their examination in advance of taking it if they were willing to part with $50. This was something that clearly infuriated Roosevelt. He requested that three officials be sacked and one be taken to court for their role in the affair.

This approach was something that the media at the time lapped up, as they applauded him for not only identifying problems, but also pushing for reform. However, the corruption in the customs house was only a relatively small issue compared to the one that he had to address at the Post Office, which involved corruption on a huge scale.

Roosevelt became aware of an issue that had existed in the Post Office in the six weeks between President Harrison being appointed to the White House and Roosevelt himself being given his position on the commission. Being a postmaster at this time was a political position that held more sway than it does today, so Roosevelt was stunned when he discovered that a staggering 30,000 fourth class postmasters had been removed from their jobs and replaced by Republicans at the behest of one individual. This meant that he now had a problem with one person by the name of John Wanamaker, who was the latest postmaster general and who had been given this position as a direct result of the spoils system. He too had been supportive of President Harrison during his campaign, and this support had led to him being given this rather important job.

It was difficult to make a case for adequate reforms that would make this kind of action impossible. But after hearing of potential corruption in Indianapolis, the home city of President Harrison, the Commission was given its opportunity.

The fact that Roosevelt had interfered only managed to irritate Wanamaker, who set out to get back at Roosevelt for crossing into his territory. Consequently, when another postmaster under scrutiny fired an individual that Roosevelt had vowed to protect, Roosevelt asked Wanamaker to intervene, and he refused to do so.

Roosevelt would continue to remain in the position even after the election of 1892 when Harrison lost to Cleveland, who still felt that Roosevelt was the best person for the job. He was put back into his position, which must have given him a major confidence boost.

It seems that Roosevelt was quite content in this job, as he was able to achieve what he had always set out to do: attempt to make a difference to people, rather than being paid vast sums of money.

1894 – A Missed Opportunity

After several years working for the Commission, and with a number of hits and misses, a number of Republicans tried to convince Roosevelt that he should once again run for the position of mayor of New York City. However, it was something the he initially had no interest in doing, although this was connected more to the reluctance of his wife to move from Washington.

For Roosevelt, this was a decision that he would ultimately come to regret, as he believed that he should have taken the opportunity to begin to work his way back into the world of politics.

The irony of it all was that by 1895 the Roosevelt family found themselves back in New York City after Roosevelt was invited to become the New York Police Commissioner. In just two years he sought to revolutionize the police force, which he also saw as having a problem with corruption.

Roosevelt came to the conclusion that he had to tackle problems from a number of angles. He would also go on to develop a reputation of walking the streets in the evening simply to make sure that people were doing their job, which appears to be something that very few before him had ever thought of doing.

The problem for Roosevelt was that the New York Police Department had long been seen as being one of the most corrupt in the country. This meant that he would be forced into potentially making wholesale changes to the way in which it operated, but this was not something that he was afraid to do.

Upon his appointment, Roosevelt adopted his usual stance with any job that he was given by throwing himself into it and giving it his all. He would actually go on to achieve a certain sense of fame through his exploits, although this also came with a price. His achievements and attempts to root out corruption led to a number of important individuals trying their absolute best to force him out of his position. Roosevelt would ultimately be attacked in a number of ways including by politicians that were being affected by his actions, as well as by those police officers that had managed to earn an impressive amount of money thanks to being corrupt.

By 1897 it felt as if everybody was gunning for him, and it became extremely difficult to do his job. However, he was rescued from what was becoming an ever increasingly difficult situation by the President of the time, William McKinley.

Assistant Secretary to the Navy

1897 saw President McKinley deciding to appoint Roosevelt to a new position as the assistant secretary to the Navy. It had long been known that Roosevelt was of the persuasion that it was extremely important for the United States to have a strong navy and the president believed that he would be just the man to stir things up and make sure that this became a reality.

However, it seems that the decision to give this position to Roosevelt was not purely on the shoulders of the president. Instead, he was persuaded by a number of prominent Republicans who believed that Roosevelt was the correct person for the job.

The problem for McKinley was that he believed the problem with Roosevelt was his natural ability to get into arguments with anybody and everybody. He was concerned that this would get in his way of making the changes that were required. In addition, McKinley was of the opinion that everything had to be done to prevent the U.S. from being drawn into conflicts abroad or problems in other countries, which was the complete opposite to how Roosevelt felt about the same situation.

As was the norm for Roosevelt, he started off at a frenetic pace in his new job, and he made it clear that he was not going to sit behind a desk and just pick up his pay each month. Instead, he made a major push for the navy to grow in both size as well as stature. He made a habit of touring the navy and spending time examining the various battleships and fleets. He tried to pick up some support for improving the fire power available to them. However, for many this was seen as being an aggressive stance to take, against the wishes of some individuals within government.

By 1898, Cuba was still in the hands of the Spanish and news reached the U.S. of revolutionaries in Cuba being executed by the Spanish. It was felt by many within the country that this was not acceptable. Roosevelt found himself at the forefront of a push to go to war against the Spanish in order to save Cuba. This was not the first time that Roosevelt had made his feelings on war clear, as he had spoken up in favor of it in 1897 when he was quoted as saying:

'No triumph of peace is quite so great as the supreme triumphs of war... It may be that at some time in the future of the race the need for war will vanish; but that time is yet ages distant. As yet no nation can hold its place in the world, or can do any work really worth doing, unless it stands ready to guard its rights with an armed hand.'

While this is not full on chest-thumping rhetoric, it is still a case of Roosevelt making his feelings on war pretty clear. The fact that he was then pushing for such an event is hardly ground breaking.

The important point to remember here is that Roosevelt was not the sole voice when it came to believing that the United States had to take action. Indeed, he was merely stating what the vast majority of the population were saying. Once again he was regarded as siding with the people, although this was hardly going to be a bad thing for him.

The reasons people felt this way were rather more complicated than solidarity with Cuba. The U.S. had gone through a period of major industrialization and they believed that this would be the perfect opportunity to show the world that the U.S. was a major world power with a vast amount of military strength. In order words, it was time to tell the world that the U.S. had arrived.

Indeed, what we see at this time is a perfect example of the way in which Roosevelt was capable of going with his gut feeling and taking control even when he was perhaps not fully intended to do so. This can be seen quite clearly when the USS Maine exploded near Havana and killed 250 American servicemen. Some claimed it was an accident, but Roosevelt was of a different opinion whereby he believed that it had been sunk by the Spanish. As a result, he took it upon himself to contact commanders in the navy in order to tell them to prepare for war against the Spanish, even though there had been no word on it from either his boss or the President.

This approach was regarded as a blatant abuse of his power, which was something that would not be approved of by others in government. However, thanks to pressure from a number of areas, President McKinley finally relented and declared war on the Spanish, much to the delight of Roosevelt.

This desire to drive a country into a war, or at least to flex their military muscle, was something that would often be linked to Roosevelt throughout his career. This in itself makes it even more surprising that he was then able to win the Nobel Peace Prize, which we will cover later on.

The Spanish-American War

The idea of being able to prove his worth on the battlefield was something that undoubtedly excited Roosevelt. However, he did not want to just sit back at some desk; he wanted to be involved in the heart of the action. Thanks to his political influence he was given permission to create his own voluntary force to send to Cuba. This was something that to us today would be a crazy idea, but he was deadly serious about trying to gain some military experience, although to lead a group of men when he had basically no idea as to what he was doing was perhaps one of his craziest ideas.

There was only one thing more surprising, and that was the fact that he was given permission by Congress to actually create this force. Quite what they were expecting, or indeed hoping would happen, is a mystery.

Roosevelt sought to create a force made up of everyone from cowboys he knew from his time in Dakota, to Harvard graduates. They did eventually make it to Cuba, but it seems as if Roosevelt was on his very own personal mission; he showed crazy levels of courage even when bullets were flying past his men. He was of the opinion that there had never been a Spanish bullet made up until this point that was capable of killing him. To some, this was not so much bravado, but rather something verging on insanity.

Roosevelt could actually be accused of being slightly reckless when it came to leading his men. They had been given the task of securing a vitally important hill called San Juan Hill, which the Spanish used to overlook the harbor at Santiago. Reports from the time state that Roosevelt lined up his troops and was so excited at advancing up the hill that he forgot to tell them to charge and ran off himself with his guns blazing. He then had to stop and look behind himself only to find that everybody else was standing around waiting for their orders. He thought they were being cowards, but in actual fact they were just being disciplined.

The very idea of any military leader conducting a charge without giving the order is astonishing. It is clear that Theodore Roosevelt was caught up in his own world at this point, as if he was living out some kind of fantasy life. The fact that anybody managed to survive with their lives intact after his command can be regarded as something akin to a miracle.

After successfully taking the hill, Roosevelt was said to be ecstatic. However, for others, he was clearly a man that was not fit to take charge of other men, as his troops had suffered in the region of seven times the number of casualties of any other regiment in the war. This was directly attributed to the way in which he led them, but Roosevelt held a different opinion. To him, it was not a sign of him being reckless in the way that he led his troops, but rather it showed how brave they were, to take on such a strong enemy with absolute and complete courage.

At the end of the day, the American public sided with Roosevelt, and through his own bravado he became a hero to the general public, which would stand him in good stead in the not too distant future. However, purists of military attacks and advances would have been well within their rights to be concerned about Roosevelt one day being in charge of the entire armed forces of the United States, after he acted so recklessly on such a small scale.

This event in Cuba would help to propel him closer to the White House, with things changing almost the instant that he landed back on American soil. However, nobody would be able to guess just quite how dramatic the change was going to be.

Chapter 6: His Road to the White House

Considering Roosevelt had effectively been out of politics for a number of years, he discovered that he was not short of offers for other jobs after the war in Cuba. However, one job would continually be put to him by the media. He was asked whether or not he was interested in running for the position of the governor of New York. The reason why this job was of interest to him was obvious, as he had held a number of important positions in and around the city, and had of course been working in the Assembly for a number of years earlier on in his career.

At first he disputed that he was interested, and indeed he would spend time fending off questions related to it, turning attention to his regiment and their success in the war. This was just a smoke screen, because Roosevelt was indeed extremely interested in trying to be elected as the governor, even though he was afraid to admit it.

The problem for Roosevelt was that he had to get the blessing of the individual that was regarded as being the most prominent Republican in the area, Senator Thomas Platt. This was not going to be easy to achieve as Platt had made it clear that he was not the biggest fan of a number of the policies or attempts at reform that had been pushed forward by Roosevelt. Indeed it was felt that he would have been quite content for anybody else to be governor rather than him.

Platt was faced with a dilemma. The current governor, Frank Black, was a Republican, but he was also known to be corrupt, and the Senator could hardly be seen to side with him. Instead, he had no real option but to opt for Roosevelt, as he was at least a man of the people, and it would reduce the chances of the Democrats winning the election, which was one thing he had to avoid at all costs. Indeed, even a reporter at the time stated:

"Platt sincerely hated him, but the Senator was a politician, and he knew that his best chance of carrying the state was to have Teddy lead his ticket."[9]

This nomination opened the door for Roosevelt. He embarked on a rigorous round of campaigning and threw everything at it. Ultimately it proved to be a success, with him winning the office of governor in 1899 at the age of 40. Little did he realize that he would be in the White House as President shortly thereafter.

The fact that he was governor did not make his life easier. Indeed, he had a major problem, in that Platt had control of a number of votes in the Legislature, so he had to solve the issue of Platt having a blatant distrust and hatred of him. The

---

[9] . Quote from Elish P. 46.

two had to work together to come to some kind of resolution for the sake of the state, and that would not be easy to achieve.

Matters were made worse when Platt announced who he wanted to be in charge of a government department, when Roosevelt was the one whose job it was to make that decision. Platt was making an attempt to force the issue and to flex his political muscle, but Roosevelt was having none of it. To him, he was the one that was in charge of this particular administration, and this meant that only he was going to be making those kinds of selections.

The problem was further exacerbated for Roosevelt by the simple fact that people he asked to take up the role had already been made aware that Platt had made his decision. This meant that they did not wish to be seen to contradict or go against the senator. He held so much power that they believed this would be career suicide. This led to everybody that Roosevelt asked turning down the opportunity, putting Roosevelt in an extremely difficult situation.

However, one thing that we have to say about him is that he was a resourceful individual. He made it clear that he was not about to be undone by this, leading to him creating a shortlist of four people that he wished to be given the position. He then presented the list to the senator and asked him to make his decision from that list. This was seen as being the perfect solution, as it meant both men were able to effectively save face. It was the perfect outcome and is a prime example of how Roosevelt was able to weave his way through the political world.

At this point, we should return to one of the most pressing issues that was always a concern for Roosevelt, the power that was held by businesses. He had the opinion that they were far too powerful for their own good and that this was wrong. He saw them as abusing their position on a regular basis. Everyday people were suffering as a result.

He saw various companies growing at an amazing speed and building their wealth in the process. However, this wealth was not filtering down to those individuals that were responsible for the boom in business in the first place, the workers.

This led to him putting forward a bill in 1899 that would change the way in which the business world dealt with their workers. Instead, businesses were forced into providing certain services, not just to their workers, but the community in general, so that everybody was able to benefit in some way. Roosevelt then faced instant rebellion, mainly from Platt, who saw it as an attempt to destroy business, although Roosevelt was adamant that he was on the correct path and forced the bill through. This can be seen as a real starting point, not only for the reforms that Roosevelt had been desperate to push through, but also for him further cementing his reputation.

Roosevelt and Reforms as Governor

Theodore Roosevelt would only be the Governor for a total of two years, but during that time he was responsible for a number of changes that would completely alter society. His main focus was on the life of the worker. He introduced an eight hour working day and forced through bills that improved the quality of living conditions for workers and the poor. At the same time, he sought to strengthen laws connected to the Civil Service in the State. As you can imagine, Roosevelt was becoming an extremely popular individual throughout the state of New York.

His increasing popularity was becoming a major issue for Platt, who already had problems with him to begin with. He understood that Roosevelt would walk away with the election when it came to nominations, and he was determined to prevent it. He was unable to convince Roosevelt to play ball, and yet if he simply refused to give him the nomination, he would be committing political suicide.

This is the part where luck was really on the side of Roosevelt. Platt eventually played a role in shaping the rest of his life, simply because of his own desire to get rid of him. He convinced the president that Roosevelt should become vice-president, in order to remove him from his current office.

This entire possibility came about due to the existing vice-president, Garret Hobart, dying of heart failure while in office. This left an opening, and Platt was sharp enough to see that he would be able to take advantage of this. He knew that the president would be forced into making a decision quickly, due to elections, and Platt was only too happy to bang the drum of Roosevelt as if he was his best political ally.

This may have sounded like a good plan, but at the turn of the century the role of vice-president was just not as powerful as it is today. Indeed, it was seen as being a position of no real power or influence. It was not something that was of interest to Roosevelt. Instead, he wanted to be in a position where he could change the lives of individuals, and he would not be able to do that if he went back to Washington.

At the end of the day, Roosevelt came to the conclusion that it was his duty to accept the nomination for the role of vice-president, due to the way he felt about the country. However, there was clearly another thought in the back of his mind. He knew that if he became the vice-president it would mean that in 1904 he would be the frontrunner for the Republican nomination for the Presidency. It seemed logical to act as the Vice-President and put up with having less power for several years if it meant that he would be able to work his way into the top job after it.

There was only one vote against his nomination, thanks to the influence of Platt, and that vote came from Roosevelt himself. In other words, it was a sweeping victory for the one man that did not want to even be victorious.

Upon his acceptance of the nomination, Roosevelt took it upon himself to go on the campaign trail. Indeed, it is noted that he would often give up to nine speeches in a single day as part of the campaign, working tirelessly to make sure that they did indeed win the election. McKinley was re-elected and Roosevelt found himself heading back to Washington in order to help to govern the country.

Roosevelt as Vice-President and then a Life Changing Event

Theodore Roosevelt was sworn in as the Vice-President in March 1901. Unbeknownst to him, his time in this position would be much shorter than anybody would have imagined.

In his position as the Vice-President, he oversaw the Senate, but did so for only a week before they stopped for the summer break. However, he had completed his time as the second in command.

The life of not only Theodore Roosevelt, but of everyone in the entire United States, would change in September of 1901, with the assassination of President McKinley.

The President had been attending an exhibition in Buffalo, when an anarchist by the name of Leon Czolgosz shot him twice in the chest. McKinley survived being shot, but soon died from his injuries. At that time, Roosevelt was on vacation. At the young age of 42, he found himself being sworn into the role of President of the United States the following day.

Roosevelt as President

Considering the way in which he found himself being pushed into the position, it should still come as no surprise to discover that Roosevelt threw himself into the job with his usual gusto. It seemed he was tailor-made for the position, and there was a sense of real freedom surrounding the way in which he approached the job. Now was the time for him to make those substantial reforms that he had been fighting for throughout his career up until this point.

Regarding his presidency, Roosevelt sought to take a moral stance. He sought to use the powers that were available to him in different ways to those that had gone before him. Too often, previous presidents appeared to bow down to various pressures. Roosevelt had been campaigning about this for some time, and did not intend to follow suit.

It is fair to say that reformists in government, and in the country as a whole, were more than happy that Roosevelt had taken over as President. They had long regarded the presidency as being too stagnant and unable to make the changes that were required to push the country forward. Now things were going to be different.

However, the business world recoiled in horror at the fact that the one individual that had been going after them for years was now in the top job. All they could see were bleak times ahead, whereby their ability to control much of the country was going to be diminished in a short period of time.

The United States that Roosevelt inherited was a country that was in a rather healthy state. Production was at an all time high, and the economy far outstripped every other country in the world. Indeed, the U.S. was producing so much in the way of various goods that the country itself was only able to consume a small percentage, with the rest being sent out as cheap exports around the world.

Roosevelt focused on four main areas during his time as President, but in each area Congress got in the way of the progress that he was hoping for. He came to the conclusion that the only way he would be able to make changes was by encouraging the public to get involved.

This idea of virtue was not exactly something new, but Roosevelt took the concept further by stressing how there was a need for private individuals to lead virtuous lives. The only way that this could be done, in his eyes, was for them to rebel against industry and to stand up against those that wished to exploit them. They had to want to live a life whereby they would no longer have to worry about where they would get food from, or the quality of their shelter. He looked to enforce the community. However, he made sure that the community that was driving this was the government, led by himself.

As a result, Roosevelt felt the need during his presidency to push forward an idea that could only be seen as being a brand new type of nationalism. The concept that he wished to stress was that the American people not only deserved to no longer have these various fears, but it was part of their right as an American to no longer have them.

At first, this sounds like something that no president would wish to interfere with, but for Roosevelt there was a problem. Indeed, these problems would form the basis of his domestic policies.

Chapter 7: His Domestic Policies

After reaching the White House, Theodore Roosevelt embarked on a number of policies on the domestic front that have really managed to cement his place as one of the most popular Presidents of all time.

The first change that should be discussed was the way in which he forced change on Congress to allow the President to have more power. We will discuss this point again when we look at his legacy and impact as President, but it is important for us to stress just how big a change this was for American politics.

Congress had previously held all of the cards in the political sphere, but change had been afoot for some time, albeit with some resistance from Congress itself. However, Roosevelt would not allow the president to be constantly usurped by Congress.

To him, there was only one option, and that was to change the way in which the president could use various powers to enforce change, even when there was no agreement from other people involved. He intended to claim the executive powers reserved to the president in the Constitution.

It is no surprise that after forcing through specific changes in this area that Roosevelt himself then sought to use them wherever he could. The president felt that he had no option but to do this, simply because of the size of the problems that he believed he had to face during his term in office.

There is no doubt that the United States had changed quite drastically over the previous few decades. For example, it is known that the population of the country had managed to double between 1870 and 1890, and clearly this in itself would have a major impact on the way in which Roosevelt would need to tackle domestic issues.

In addition, the U.S. was becoming more industrial, and cities were becoming larger, as the country was moving from being rural to urban. Yet again, this would have an impact on the way in which Roosevelt would then need to run the country.

However, even though this may have sounded positive, the truth of the matter is that this was not the case. Instead, what Roosevelt saw was an increase in the amount of overcrowding in the cities, leading to issues with infrastructure and accommodation, as well as poor working conditions, big business having too much of a say in both the economy and politics, and an unbalanced economy.

Addressing Concerns About Society

One of the first areas giving Roosevelt cause for concern was the influence that big business appeared to hold over society, and in particular, politics. For him, this was an issue that had to be addressed, as Roosevelt was well aware of the simple fact that the people were becoming tired of powerful businesses.

However, he also held the belief that you had to have big business on your side, as they were the driving force behind allowing the economy to develop, so he was stuck somewhat in the middle. To Roosevelt, the economy was more important than virtually anything else, as he knew that the economy had to grow to allow additional changes that would improve the rest of society. He came to the conclusion that he was not able to actively tackle the issue of business, as he had to look at the bigger picture.

Any president has to look at the concept of reforms and Roosevelt was no different. However, he felt that there was no need to make major fundamental changes to either society or the economy. This was a tough position for him, because he also understood that there was a real need for reforms, due to the rise of socialism across the country. This, to him, posed dangers for the entire country. In short, the government had to take some kind of action, to keep the population from taking more drastic ones.

Furthermore, Roosevelt came into office in unusual circumstances, due to the assassination of McKinley. Roosevelt was a wonderful politician in that he understood that he had to create some kind of continuity, as the country was in a state of shock after the assassination. He came to the initial conclusion that his early domestic policies had to show some kind of continuation, as the country was in a form of mourning.

This was something that could only go on for a short period of time, as he had his own thoughts as to policies that should be implemented.

Roosevelt held the opinion that the president was effectively the "steward" of the country. This was a feeling that he had held since his initial nomination for the vice-presidency. He took this stance as he saw that only the president and the vice-president were democratically elected into the position of head of government. He then took his job extremely seriously as he did hold the belief that he was duty bound to the people of the country and he was required to do everything in his power to make sure that he met their expectations.

In addition, he held the belief that this was the reason why the president was required to have additional powers; he had to be seen as being capable of acting immediately if a situation required him to do so. The citizens of the country would look to him for actions to be taken in a time of crisis. If he had to go back to Congress discuss it, then in his eyes he was unable to do the job for which he was elected. This may sound like something straightforward, but it was actually capable of shaking the government to its very core when he put forward this argument.

However, he did make it clear that he never wanted his new powers to directly contravene any laws or the Constitution. He was helped by changes to the law that were introduced by the Supreme Court before he was even made President, whereby they broadened the meaning of presidential powers.

For example, we can turn to aspects of the foreign policy of the United States, which notes that treaties or international agreements had to be passed by Congress as long as two-thirds of the Senators voted in accordance with the treaty. However, Roosevelt came to the conclusion that he was actually able to get around this by using the powers of the executive agreement. This was completely different, in that it was an agreement between the president and the government of another country. In other words, this did not require the consent of Congress for things to be passed allowing him to make agreements abroad without talking to anybody else about it.

Changes to Business

As we stated in the previous chapter, the United States economy was booming to such an extent that the population was unable to consume even a fraction of the items being produced. The net worth of the entire country was also huge, $25 billion greater than the country in second place.[10] With everything appearing rosy, it is perhaps no surprise that the business world was rather worried about Roosevelt moving into the White House.

One of the main bones of contention for Roosevelt was that the concept of there being a free market was rather idealistic within the United States. It is true that for decades there was a fair economy whereby everybody had the

---

[10] . According to Elish P 52.

opportunity of making money, but things had changed over the previous decade or so.

Instead, what had once been a fair and competitive market had been replaced by a handful of companies simply becoming too powerful within their industry, meaning they were able to create a monopoly on the production of goods, the workers and the price that products could sell for. This was something that was strongly against what Roosevelt believed in.

Indeed, to show how bad the situation was, we only have to look at the oil industry in the 1890's in the US. The industry had, of course, been important for some time, but in the 1890's almost 90% of it was under the control of just one individual, John D. Rockefeller.

There had been attempts by President Harrison to change this, but company owners simply grew to be too clever, and would change their companies to form trusts in order to circumvent the new laws that were in place. Changing this would eventually lead to America as a whole changing.

Even though he did understand that he had to be careful with how he handled business, he was aware that changes had to be made regarding the influence that it had on society. This eventually led to one of his main domestic policies, whereby he believed that the government should be in a position where it was able to regulate business when it was for the sake of society. This is where he began to develop his reputation as being "the great regulator".

In order to carry out these changes, Roosevelt sought to use a law that had been passed in 1890 that had only been used extremely sparingly since then. The law in question was the Sherman Antitrust Act. Shock waves were felt across the nation when it was brought into effect by the government in 1902 against the Northern Securities Company.

This first instance of it being used was brought about by the Department of Justice, but it did signal the intent of the administration to bring business to task for its failures.

The reason why this act was used in this instance was relatively easy to understand. The company in question was a huge conglomeration of various wealthy and powerful individuals and companies that had come together for the sake of the railroad. However, in the eyes of the government, it was merely a monopoly, and was crushing those that may have been trying to gain a foothold in the business. The mere fact that this act had been used may have initially scared the business world, but they would have still been of the opinion that it would blow over and Roosevelt would go back to the more hands off approach that had been used by his predecessors. This would not be the case especially when the US Supreme Court ruled in favor of the government in 1904 with the result being that the entire company was forced into being disbanded.

Turning to the Railroad

The success of the case against the Northern Securities Company put the rest of the business world on notice. They had to watch how they operated, or else the government would take steps to reduce the level of power that they were able to wield. However, Roosevelt and his administration were not finished. They would go and turn their attention to one industry that had seen major expansion: the railroads.

The fact that they turned to this industry should really come as no surprise when you consider what the Northern Securities Company was involved in. It appears that the government only became interested after being informed of abuses taking place. The institute behind these allegations was the Interstate Commerce Commission; they informed the government that substantial abuse was taking place in the industry that was affecting its effectiveness.

Furthermore, normal people were making it pretty clear that they too felt that something had to be done to tackle the railroads, as they believed that they were not operating in a way that benefited the economy. Indeed, a number of people and businesses relied heavily on the railroad, so it became clear to Roosevelt that something had to be done to tackle the abuse.

His first attempt at resolving the issues came in 1903 with the creation of the Elkins Act. The idea behind this act was that it prevented the railroad companies from giving preferential rates to certain companies. This was regarded as being unfair to business and that the rates should have been the same rate for everybody.

This special rebate for big businesses meant they were then able to ship their products cheaper. This meant that they had an unfair advantage over smaller businesses, putting them at risk of going out of business.

The very fact that Roosevelt had attempted to tackle such a huge conglomerate within a matter of months of assuming the position of president was something that threw the business world into disarray. Indeed, a newspaper report from the time stated how:

"Wall Street is paralyzed at a thought that a president of the United States should sink so low as to try to enforce the law."[11]

Now, that quote may be slightly tongue in cheek, but it is perhaps closer to the truth than we realize. For decades large businesses had been getting away with anything that they chose to do

---

[11] . Quote from Elish P 54.

and nobody appeared to be ready to try to stop them. They realized relatively early on that Roosevelt was not going to play ball. There must have been a sense of wondering who would be targeted next.

However, the act, and indeed Roosevelt's initial attempts at changing the business world, was not as effective as it should have been, as both the companies and railroad were able to circumvent the act to make sure that they were able to continue to offer rebates. This infuriated Roosevelt, who realized that he was effectively being taken for a ride by business. This would eventually lead to one of the major domestic policies of his time as president, the Hepburn Act.

The Creation of the Hepburn Act

The Hepburn Act was created specifically to stop large businesses and the railroad companies coming together for their mutual benefit.

The basic concept of this act was that the Interstate Commerce Commission was to have its powers increased. Their new powers included setting shipping rates for the railroad. However, Roosevelt ran into problems, as there were further issues, whereby the courts had to come to some kind of a conclusion as to the different rates.

Furthermore, there were issues within the Senate, especially with the Conservatives, who had vigorously opposed the idea of increasing the power of the ICC. They were linked to the railroad companies as well as to big business, so their desire to oppose the idea does seem obvious. Their idea was that the courts should rule on individual cases, rather than there being a blanket ruling. This in itself was regarded as being a clever move on the part of the Conservatives, as it also meant that the ICC saw its powers being undermined immediately.

Once again, Roosevelt was furious at the attempt to crush one of his policies by members of Congress. He then felt the need to determine what the public thought of the issue. He would mention it time and time again in various speeches in order to gauge feedback from the public.

This is the reason why the Hepburn Act is seen as being so important. It was the first time that the president used the power of the people to get a bill or act passed.

Balancing the Economy and Social Justice

Due in part to his desire to improve society in general, Roosevelt felt the need for the government to become involved in a number of instances where it was believed that the economy and welfare of the people was in danger.

One such example came in 1902 when there was a shortage of coal, leading to problems developing across the country. This particular problem was exacerbated by the onset of winter.

It has to be stressed that at this moment the government had no official power to end a strike, so Roosevelt was left with few options. It was his idea to bring together both parties to determine if a deal could be struck, but the management of the mine initially refused to enter into any negotiations.

This refusal to enter negotiations was seen by Roosevelt as a slight on him, although he steadfastly refused to accept that this was the end of the matter.

The management may have been led to believe that the government would side with them and ultimately use the army to force the workers back to work. However, this would not be the case. Instead, Roosevelt put forward the suggestion that if there was no progress from the side of the management, he would send in the troops to take control of the mines and run them as a Federal business.

This threat was enough to break the deadlock, with both parties stating that they were quite content to allow an independent commission to look at their claims and issues and to go along with whatever suggestions they made. In other words, the mere threat of losing control was enough to change things, and this ultimately led to an agreement that Roosevelt felt was fair to everybody.

The reason why this incident is mentioned is because it is a prime example of the way in which Roosevelt would seek to deal with domestic issues. In his opinion, it was important that everybody felt that they had gained in some way, or else the issues could never be adequately resolved. This approach became known as the "square deal" and it was something that was recurring throughout his time as president.

This square deal idea was something that could be applied in various industries. It helped to balance out every argument, no matter if it was the workers against management, the business world against the end consumer, or even the developer against conservationists.

On the face of it, this approach had potential, but Roosevelt himself was honest enough to admit that it did need some adjustment for it to be as effective as it should be. In his mind, the government needed to become involved on a more constant basis, in order to protect the end consumer who was often the one that lost out in these disputes.

His Models of Government Connected to the Economy

The economy was central to a number of changes that Roosevelt was attempting to make to the American society, but he was not a fan of the Jefferson concept of limited government.

Instead, he preferred to adopt what was known as the Hamiltonian model, whereby the real focus was on having an extremely strong government at the heart of the country.

Roosevelt was aware that the United States economy was rather complex in nature and that it would more than likely only continue to get worse as it grew. In his opinion, the only way in which this complex economy could ever hope to be regulated in any manner was via a very strong federal government that understood its powers and was not afraid to use them.

His approach was one that would ultimately be taken up by those that followed him, but he was seen as being quite radical in his thinking at this point. He was not afraid to unsettle the business world if required to do so. One area that was of particular concern to him was the way in which those governments before him had lacked the apparent authority, or will power, to change and regulate trade. This had allowed larger businesses to take control and to limit the free market.

We stated earlier how big business was afraid of what would happen when Roosevelt came to power, but he was not crazy in his approach. There was an understanding that he had to find that intricate balance between helping the workers and making sure that he did not destroy the economy by hitting big businesses too hard and too soon.

The Government as the Go-Between

One of the first areas in which Roosevelt sought to make a difference was by installing the government as a negotiator between company and worker. For too long Roosevelt was of the opinion that workers were simply being abused, as they were unaware of their rights or were too scared to take action because they knew they were in a poor situation to begin with. His hope was that, thanks to the government taking a key role, he would be able to encourage the companies to talk and come to some kind of a resolution.

Tackling Monopolies and Trusts

By 1901, the public opinion of monopolies and trusts was that they were bad for the country. However, some believed they were able to increase the efficiency of the economy and that they had to largely be left alone for fear of what may happen if they were broken up. This was not the approach that Roosevelt took. He, along with a number of other prominent individuals, believed that this would only lead to major issues in the economy with higher prices due to the lack of competition.

The problem he had was that it was impossible, and not a good idea from a political point of view, to tackle every single monopoly that existed. Instead, he sought to find some kind of middle ground whereby he could be seen to be taken action on both sides.

His approach was to look at the different monopolies and to come to some kind of a conclusion as to which ones were more abusive than others. He believed that by at least breaking up those that were more hated, it would show the public that he was serious.

He made economic reform the central part of his State of the Union address in order to prepare them for what was to come. His statement made it very clear indeed as to his feelings on this entire matter.

"the tremendous and highly complex industrial development which went on with ever accelerated rapidity during the latter half of the nineteenth century brings us face to face...with very serious social problems. The old laws, and the old customs...were once quite sufficient to

regulate the accumulation and distribution of wealth...they are no longer sufficient."[12]
He continued, saying how change had to be made and that he was seeking for the government to be given additional powers to allow them to make changes when it came to regulating the economy.

Dealing with Trusts

We mentioned briefly how Roosevelt felt that he had to tackle the issue of monopolies and trusts and the point regarding trusts is in itself rather important. The very existence of them only came around due to those involved in businesses trying their best to avoid laws that had been introduced to dissolve monopolies. Their approach was to break up those large companies and to then seek to create a number of apparently smaller companies that were run by

---

[12] _Quote from Hunt P 127.

the same board. They were the same company, just under a different guise.

This infuriated the president, who vowed that he would tackle such a practice as he saw it as a slight on himself. He began by warning such trusts that they were required to stop those business practices that were deemed to be abusive, or they would face dire consequences.

In order to help himself push through this idea of tackling the trusts, Roosevelt went back to the bully pulpit principle and spent time gathering public support, which was relatively easy to do considering so many people were simply fed up with the trusts as well. Due to this, he saw a huge increase in the level of support that he held in both the working and middle class of America. They viewed him as a U.S. President that was actually capable of working for the people rather than being swayed by money or power. They saw him as being a people person, since he was making honest attempts to improve their quality of life and to give them more rights than they had before. In addition, people that owned small businesses also stated that they were in support of what he was trying to do although this was clearly due to a desire for self-preservation as their own businesses were at real risk of simply being swallowed up.

The problem for Roosevelt was that the only real opposition that he faced for tackling the issue of the trusts was from Congress, since they were often linked in some way. In return, those in Congress that did oppose the concept were also in a difficult situation. Roosevelt had managed to do such a good job of gathering together support for his approach amongst the general public that Congress felt that they were unable to openly vote against it as they were fearful for their own jobs.

To help with the investigation into business, Roosevelt directly asked Congress for their help to create the Bureau of Corporations, with their sole purpose at the outset being to investigate those companies that had too much say on their part of the economy. It was the first of many such developments that would take a closer look at various aspects of the country in order to determine how they could very well be improved.

Avoiding Taking the Economy Too Far

It is important for us to note that Roosevelt did understand that he had to perform some kind of balancing act between reform and not destroying what was a healthy economy. That was why he actively campaigned against the ideas of some Democrats, who were of the opinion that Roosevelt was not going far enough regarding the way in which he attacked big business.

Indeed, Roosevelt himself felt that there were some individuals that would have effectively destroyed the country had they been allowed to carry on. As he himself worded it:

'They saw the evil done by the big combinations, and sought to remedy it by destroying them and restoring the country to the economic conditions of the middle of the nineteenth century. This was a hopeless effort.'[13]

This quote in itself is rather surprising, coming from Roosevelt, as he was always regarded as being a major reformer, and would push people to their absolute limit in order to make changes that he felt were for the good of the country. Clearly he felt that the more liberal reformers were guilty of taking things too far, so there were obviously limitations as to what he believed should happen in order to improve the country.

The Role of Conservation

---

[13] _Quote from Elish P 55.

It can also be argued that Roosevelt was the first president who was actually interested in the idea of conservation. To him, there was a need to make sure that the woodlands and nature in general was protected, especially in the face of rapid urban growth. Indeed, a number of historians have credited him as being the first conservationist president.

To him, there was a real need for a balance between using natural resources and abusing them, as there was a clear link between American culture and nature that could not be ignored. This desire led to him working closely with two powerful and influential individuals, Gifford Pinchot, who was head of forestry, as well as Frederick Newell, who was head of reclamation. By 1902, Roosevelt had signed off on the Newlands Reclamation Bill, which set out how the government was going to use funds to help protect the natural world throughout the US.

The basis of this act was that money raised from federal sales of land would then be used in some very specific ways in the west. The problem, as Roosevelt saw it, was that the west suffered from being far too arid, and for that area to grow, things had to be done regarding water. This led to the creation of reservoirs, as well as irrigation systems. However, Roosevelt still felt as if he was being restricted in what he was able to do until he was successfully re-elected of his own accord in 1904. It is important for us to remember that Roosevelt had always felt slightly handicapped when he first reached the White House due to the circumstances, so he believed that he was unable to be too proactive until the next election.

After being re-elected, Roosevelt made larger moves within this field. First, he opted to move the forestry department from the Department of the Interior to Agriculture. By doing so, he was able to provide Pinochet with more power and the ability to not only set goals, but making it easier to obtain them.

Furthermore, both Pinochet and Roosevelt were only too aware that local government, and also state government, had a tendency to deal with issues related to nature in an unfair way. He believed that things were being left wide open to corruption. It would have not come as a surprise to him when he encountered a considerable amount of resistance at the plans from those that clearly stood to miss out on so much.

To Roosevelt, there was no real argument to be had. It was obvious that only the Federal government had the ability, as well as the finances, to deal with such vast projects. Leaving it in the hands of local government would only mean that there would be a greater risk of projects not being handled correctly or not completed on time. Due to this, it should be noted that during his time as president, Theodore Roosevelt increased the number of national forests by 150 and increased the area that was protected from 42 million acres to 172 million acres. In addition, there were five brand new national parks as well as 51 new wildlife refuges and 18 national monuments.

Civil Rights and Race

The twin issues of civil rights and race had been a hotbed for discussion for some time across the United States.

When it came to issues connected to race, Roosevelt was a bit hit and miss. For example, the black population that lived in the south had long complained about being alienated from society and even though he was aware of this fact, there was virtually no attempt to change things.

This was more than likely due to Roosevelt believing that blacks were inferior to whites as a race, but he also accepted that there were a number of black individuals that were actually superior to some whites. As you can see, this comes across as being slightly contradictory in nature so it is no surprise that his policies connected to race were also as confusing.

This is not to say that he was unfriendly towards black people, but he also made it extremely clear that he did not have the political willpower to fight the various causes that black people were tackling in order to gain equal rights.

Roosevelt invited Dr. Booker T. Washington to the White House not long after becoming President. This invitation was significant, as Washington was a prominent African American within the world of education and his presence in the White House was seen as being a major scandal at the time. Indeed, a newspaper even commented on it being an absolute outrage and the most shocking thing ever done by a citizen of the United States.

It should be noted that Roosevelt did not put race relations at the forefront of his political policies, but he was willing to stand up for the rights of African Americans when he was required to do so. In Indianola in 1903 an African American Post Mistress was forced to resign from her position simply because she had become too wealthy in the eyes of others. However, Roosevelt not only blocked her from being sacked, but re-instated her on her full salary and closed her Post Office. If this was seen as being a rather strange act, then it was merely Roosevelt making the point that anybody could, and should, be considered for the position, and if they were a success then they were to be left alone and not punished simply because of their skin.

If we now look at the concept of civil rights, one important area for him was an attempt to lower the age at which veterans were able to obtain their pension. He wished to lower the age to 62, but he was blocked by Congress, which claimed that it was simply unable to justify the huge cost that would be incurred by this. Their actions infuriated Roosevelt, who was only too aware of the simple fact that there were a number of veterans who were in their 60's and were unable to earn a living due to ill health. He saw this as a real injustice and set out to attempt to change it for the better.

This in itself is another example of the way in which he used the executive powers granted to him as president. As we said, he was annoyed by the way in which Congress blocked his plans, so he changed it himself thanks to an executive order. This act left Congress in uproar, as many saw Roosevelt as abusing his power. With this example, he was able to irritate both sides of the political divide as even his fellow Republicans felt that he had overstepped the mark.

The Bully Pulpit

Upon his inauguration, Roosevelt had stated that he would be trying to continue with a number of the policies that had been put forward in the election campaign by President McKinley.

Roosevelt had come to the conclusion that they had both won the election due to those promises, so he felt duty bound to follow through with them wherever possible. However, he also made it abundantly clear that it did not mean that he was going to abandon his ideas of pushing through reforms. Indeed, the complete opposite would be true.

What became clear early on with his domestic policies was his willingness to use all of his powers, especially when it came to issues where he felt there was a moral obligation for him to act as president. He had a distinctive style when dealing with various problems and he was very different in his approach compared to McKinley. People began to refer to his style as bullying, as he was able to somehow conjure up support across the country for his policies even when Congress was largely against him.

The fact that he had to adopt this policy did come as a surprise to some, as the Republicans controlled both Houses, but there was no point where Roosevelt believed that he was able to wield his power without mercy. Instead, he would often come up against opposition from those within his own party.

In order to help his position, Roosevelt had come to the conclusion that the press could be used to his advantage. The media was gradually becoming more powerful than before, and he was of the opinion that he could utilize this power to push through those policies that were being swamped in the quagmire of Congress.

He was intelligent enough to know that he had to get them on his side. That can perhaps explain why he was the first president to give the press their very own room in the White House, making it easier for them to find out what was going on. In addition, he installed telephone lines, which were still a new invention, to make sure that the press corps of the White House could send out the story from the government before anybody else was able to. In effect, he sped up the rate at which news could be sent out and forever changed the way in which the media would report on the affairs of the President.

Furthermore, Roosevelt would take things further with the press by inviting key members out to lunch in order to get their feedback on a variety of issues of the day. However, he was also known to take certain reporters to task that disappointed him with what they published in their newspaper so it was not all one sided. As a punishment, he would ban them from being able to obtain any further interviews until he felt that they had been suitably chastised. Considering how important it was to hear from the President, this was something that no reporter wanted to happen to them.

Finally, Roosevelt also adopted a policy whereby he would send in editorials to various newspapers if he felt that they had published a story that was either completely untrue or something he felt was misleading. His editorial was intended to set the record straight to make sure that his point was put across at all times. His attempted control of the media was not something that would have gone unnoticed by his opponents.

Tackling Food and Drugs

Roosevelt was the kind of president that did listen to the people and proof of that approach comes in the way in which he tackled issues surrounding food and drugs. The public had made it clear that they believed there had been abuse in the way in which food was being packaged, and as he felt that it was having a direct impact on their lives, he had no option but to attempt to make amends.

This ultimately led to the creation of several acts that were intended to regulate the way in which food and drugs were not only processed, but also how they were then sold to the public. In particular, he wished to address the problem of things not being labeled correctly, which ultimately led to the Meat Inspection Act of 1906. In addition, this same act meant that those companies in the food industry had to avoid using any chemicals that may be harmful to humans. The very fact that this required an act to be passed is in itself astonishing.

What is clear is that the majority of the time spent on domestic issues was focused on tackling a number of key areas: corruption, civil rights, breaking down monopolies and trusts, and conservation. Of course, there were also a number of other aspects that would change society in general and his policies were clearly aimed at cementing his reputation as being the kind of individual that was always there for the people.

Overall, his domestic policies did bring about substantial change to the extent that the economy did change for the better and fewer monopolies were able to take advantage of the economy and the way in which it was being run. He reduced corruption, although it was still rife, and workers did manage to obtain a better deal than ever before. We can therefore conclude that his domestic policies were a relative success although even Roosevelt himself would have agreed that he could have done better.

Foreign Policies

By examining his foreign policies, we get a better idea of the way in which Roosevelt approached not only the presidency, but also the diplomatic world. Even at this stage it was clear that the United States was a force to be reckoned with and this had to also be reflected in his foreign policies.

What we see when we examine his foreign policies is that they accurately reflect his own beliefs regarding the world. They would become intertwined with the way in which the United States was shown to the world. Roosevelt was relatively lucky in that the country was in a healthy state when he got to the White House although that did not stop him from trying to improve things.

Upon becoming president, Theodore Roosevelt would have noticed that he had inherited what could only be described as an empire in development. This was largely due to the Spanish-American war that had taken place in 1898. The Spanish were forced into giving not only Guam to the United States, but also Puerto Rico and the Philippines. In addition, moves had been afoot to establish more of a presence on Hawaii, and there was a protectorate over Cuba as well. In other words, the United States was spreading and the foreign policies of Roosevelt would, therefore, have greater importance than ever before.

Roosevelt viewed the world in his own unique way, but to him the most pressing issue was to make sure that he was successful in increasing the power of the United States in the world while also increasing its ability to influence other global matters. However, he was also a strong advocate of what he saw as the perfect American ideals. As a result he held the belief that by exporting the American way of doing things, and American opinions, the entire world would benefit as a result.

At the same time, Roosevelt was not an idiot. He knew that this was a time in the world where there were always risks associated with trying to increase levels of influence. He understood there was a need to make sure that the country itself was being adequately defended. He knew that the enemies of the United States would seek to exploit any sign of weakness and as a result there was a need to strengthen the defense of the country and to show the world that the United States was in a strong position.

As a direct result of this desire, Roosevelt came to the conclusion that he had to be aggressive when it came to his foreign policy. He was not afraid to threaten people with the use of force in order to make sure that the U.S. was not only respected, but also feared. Indeed, his idea of potentially using force, and not being afraid to use it, became a central aspect of his policies for dealing with the world.

It was often the case that Roosevelt was alone in his approach. Indeed, it would often result in him using his newly acquired powers to take action on various issues even without the consent of Congress and at times without them even being aware of what he intended to do.

Support for His Policies

For any president there is always the difficult task of trying to balance out domestic and foreign policies with the understanding that it is impossible for you to be viewed in a positive light by everybody.

However, that is not to say that Roosevelt was out on his own with his approach to foreign matters as he actually enjoyed some rather strong support from a number of different senators. In addition, he also managed to build a substantial amount of support from the public as well.

Supporters of his foreign policy who had also found themselves in powerful positions prior to Roosevelt getting to the White House were known to have grown closer together due to them meeting in Manhattan on a regular basis. This was seen by some as representing a potential conflict of interests for Roosevelt, who had long argued against nepotism.

Roosevelt and Imperialism

Considering the way in which Roosevelt viewed the use of military power in order to win battles, it is perhaps no surprise to discover that he held quite firm views on the issue of imperialism. He had noticed that previous presidents had got into trouble regarding Hawaii and the Philippines. Roosevelt believed that he should keep the country away from taking over new territory thanks to political conquest. Instead he had the belief that the United States should use its size and power to try to influence countries wherever possible.

In other words, he had no desire to build an empire, unlike countries in Europe that were scouring the world for land to control. He saw the idea of democracy as being the best thing that the U.S. could give the world. Roosevelt had the strong belief that he was the correct one to take this matter forward.

His Understanding of Other Countries

When looking at his foreign policies, it is useful for us to look at the way in which Roosevelt viewed other countries to get a better understanding of how he would perhaps position the United States in the world. He had a distinct feeling that there was a need to protect areas of the world, and particularly those that had a close relationship with the United States. He had a particular distrust of Germany and saw them as being the main instigator of trouble across Europe. He had no idea that he would end up being so accurate in his prediction with what followed just over a decade later.

However, his issues with Germany were perhaps more to do with them being the main competition against the United States in areas such as Asia and Latin America. For him, this was effectively stepping on the toes of the United States.

Roosevelt and Japan

When it came to his relationship with Japan, he made sure that the United States supported them in a number of different ways. The United

States and Japan worked together on a number of things, including demanding access to the Chinese market. He also joined the alliance that was formed in 1902 between Japan and the United Kingdom as he saw that it was a perfect opportunity to make some in-roads in his battle against what he determined to be the rather unhealthy rise of Germany and its allies in Europe.

Roosevelt and the Philippines

As a sign of what was to come regarding his foreign policies, we only have to look at the Philippines.

This was of course one of the lands that the United States had effectively been given by Spain after the end of the war. However, Roosevelt was of the opinion that there was practically no need to work on expanding American influence in Asia, even though he was concerned about other countries trying to do it themselves. He was adamant that he would protect the Philippines should anybody try to impose themselves on the country.

This does sum up the way in which he would actively tackle problems with other countries abroad. He had no desire to create an American empire, but he was more than happy to consolidate what they did have without enforcing anything other than a democratic rule.

Issues with Latin America

As the president of the United States, it is obvious that Roosevelt would have an interest in what was happening within Latin America. Furthermore, this was the time where there were plans afoot to create a canal and Roosevelt was understandably concerned as to how that was going to have an impact on the United States. His concerns in the area were increased even further in 1902 when several European countries sought to create a blockade of Venezuela due to their reluctance to pay back loans. Roosevelt came to the conclusion that there was a chance of other motives being behind these naval moves.

However, his ability to negotiate and to get different sides to come together came to his aid at this point. He was able to convince all of the parties involved to come together, with the United States acting as the arbitrator to make sure that they could come to some kind of an agreement. The fact that he had also managed to remove Germany from Latin America would have also given him a boost.

We mentioned that this was when the idea of building a canal in Central America came about, but there were two countries being put forward as possible locations. The first was Nicaragua; the second was Panama. Roosevelt successfully convinced Congress that it was in the best interests of the United States that the canal be built in Panama, even though Colombia rejected the idea of the canal being built there. Roosevelt then helped a rebellion to take place within the country, in order to force through the deal with a treaty then being struck. And, as we know, the Panama canal was born.

The Nobel Peace Prize

It could effectively be argued that his foreign policy was a major contributing factor towards his winning of the Nobel Peace Prize in 1905. This award came about due to him creating a peace treaty between Russia and Japan after the war that took place between the two between 1904 and 1905.

In addition, his role in Mexico of arbitrator in a disagreement also played a role for the official committee that decided who would win the prize.

Roosevelt was actually the very first statesman to win the prize, and the fact that he was to receive it was regarded as being quite controversial at the time. Indeed, some of his opponents, and by this we mean around the world and not just political opponents in the United States, claimed that he was mad about military achievements and had taken over the Philippines after it had been given to the U.S. as part of their treaty.

His reasons for becoming involved in a peace treaty between Russia and Japan was of course not done simply because he wanted everybody to get along. He held the opinion that having a strong Japan in Asia was perhaps not in the best interests for the United States, so the idea of them defeating the Russians and taking a bigger hold in this part of the world was a concern.

At the same time, he was aware that both sides had become tired of fighting after a year, so he felt that it was the perfect opportunity to carry out his concept of speaking softly but carrying a big stick to get results. In doing so, he invited both parties to visit Portsmouth in New Hampshire to work out a resolution that was going to be suitable for both countries.

The outcome, after a lot of arguing and a struggle for them to accept various concessions, was a peace deal that was signed in September of 1905. Due to this, he was awarded the peace prize, although he then donated his winnings to an organization that was involved in peace work.

The foreign policies adopted by Theodore Roosevelt summed up his approach to politics in general. He had personally stated how you had to take a soft approach to various issues, but to let the parties involved know that you had the power to do something if required.

He was able to show that he was a skilled negotiator in peace as well as pushing points through for the security of the United States.

We can conclude that his foreign policies were relatively successful and he managed to achieve most of what he set out to do. He made sure that the United States built its reputation in the world and their ability to manufacture and produce a number of goods meant that they were able to begin to formulate their position as a true superpower.

It is possible for us to come to the conclusion that the changes introduced by Roosevelt set the tone for how the United States is viewed in the world today.

Chapter 8: His Life After the Presidency

By the time we get to 1908 there were a number of people that effectively wanted Roosevelt to run for a third time as President. In the modern world this is something that is illegal, but the part of the Constitution that states no president can run for more than two elections had not yet been passed. However, there were also some individuals that held that, as Roosevelt had been promoted to the position thanks to the assassination of McKinley, he had not actually run in two different elections.

The important point was that Roosevelt himself felt that it would be wrong for him to run for a third term, as there was no tradition of it and he was not inclined to break that trend.

Even with this there was a problem. Roosevelt was rightly concerned that if he did not run, the Republican Party might fracture along the lines of those individuals that fully supported him and those that were against him. His fear was that this divide in the party would then allow the Democrats to sweep to power, and that was something that all Republicans would be united against.

In order to circumvent this potentially disastrous outcome, he came to the conclusion that he should select a successor, as this individual would then receive the backing of his supporters. As a result, and after some wrangling with the Senate, it was announced that William Taft would be the nominee for the Republicans for the presidential elections. Ultimately, Taft would win the election.

Roosevelt Becoming Unhappy with His Choice

There can be little doubt that Roosevelt had hoped he would be able to maintain some kind of control thanks to somebody that he had personally selected now being president. However, that would not be the case.

After the nomination and election, Roosevelt had traveled to Africa to embark on a safari which lasted for close to a year. Even during this extended break, Roosevelt made full use of the media with the American public thoroughly enjoying reading about the exploits of President Roosevelt as he bagged yet another kill on his trip. Once the safari was over, he then moved through Europe to deliver lectures at a number of universities before the entire family returned to the United States in 1910.

Upon his arrival back in the country, he was left open-mouthed by the way in which the country was being run under the command of President Taft. Indeed, he was stunned to discover that Taft had only succeeded in alienating those within the Republican Party that were regarded as being the Progressives, the exact thing that he had been trying to avoid in the first place. Roosevelt saw that Taft had become the type of president that would bow down to those in charge of major businesses.

For Roosevelt, there was a need to at least attempt to bring the party back together, although he did have a particular attachment to the Progressives. He then embarked on something akin to a tour around the country, giving speech after speech to party members, within which he sought to appeal to those that were wanting change.

This caused problems between Roosevelt and Taft to such an extent that their friendship came to an end. Indeed, Roosevelt was left irate when Taft forced through a lawsuit against U.S. Steel in direct contravention to promises that had been made by Roosevelt to J.P. Morgan that this would never happen. The promise had come after Morgan stated they would not allow the economy to slide after a recession. To then see Taft argue against this and push through charges was a major slap in the face to Roosevelt. He then made matters worse by doing this on Roosevelt's birthday which is perhaps no coincidence.

The Push to be President Once Again

The incident with U.S Steel convinced a number of Republicans that the only way that the party could make any progress was if Roosevelt ran for President in 1912. This was something that he was not keen to do, for the exact reasons he had rejected the idea for the 1908 election. But the Progressives within the party badgered him continuously until he gave in and stated that he would indeed fight for the nomination.

What then evolved was a rather ugly contest between the two, with both individuals being guilty of turning it into a mud-slinging match, with Roosevelt referring to Taft as being disloyal, while Taft referred to Roosevelt as being unethical.

At the Republican Party convention in Chicago there was a tense atmosphere. This was only made worse when delegates voted that Taft would be given the nomination. This immediately resulted in both Roosevelt as well as his supporters walking out and a matter of hours later they had formed what would be known as the Progressive Party. Upon its creation, Roosevelt was asked in an interview if he was even fit to run for president, at which point he replied he was as fit as a bull moose. This ultimately led to the new creation being known as the Bull Moose Party, even though this was done slightly tongue-in-cheek.

The Build-Up to the 1912 Election

In the build-up to the 1912 election there was so much attention being focused on the

Republicans and the battle between Taft and Roosevelt that it went relatively unnoticed that the Democrats had elected Woodrow Wilson as their candidate. He was regarded as being quite a progressive individual who had garnered a substantial amount of support for himself after becoming the governor of New Jersey in 1910.

The decision to run for president would almost result in Roosevelt's death, due to an attempted assassination when he appeared at a rally on October 14th, 1912 in Milwaukee. An individual by the name of John Crank shot Roosevelt in the chest, but thanks to both his physical strength as well as a metal case in his pocket, he not only survived but continued to give his speech even though there was now a bullet stuck on his chest. Crank was held by a mob at the scene, but Roosevelt instructed them not to harm him. He would never discover why Crank had wanted him dead.

The result of the election showed that Woodrow Wilson had come first, as the Republicans had split their vote between both Taft and Roosevelt. Due to their arguing, neither of them actually stood a chance. With this defeat, the newly formed Progressive Party was re-amalgamated into the Republican Party fold.

His political life came to a close after his defeat in the 1912 election to Woodrow Wilson, but for Roosevelt it marked a completely new chapter. At first, he appears to have decided that it would be the perfect time to embark on some time with his family. We know that he and his son took the decision to go on a voyage to Brazil. However, this voyage turned into an expedition that took some seven months to complete and covered approximately 15,000 miles.

For Roosevelt, it was not exactly the happiest of excursions. We know that he injured his leg in a boating incident, but the most serious part was him contracting malaria in the jungles of Brazil, a disease that could have easily killed him.

After the journey was complete, Roosevelt returned to the United States and he settled into a life of writing scientific papers along with books that were dedicated to various periods and people from history.

Roosevelt and World War I

1914 was of course an important year for the world, with the outbreak of war in Europe. Even though the United States was not yet involved in 1914, Roosevelt did feel that he had to use his influence in order to encourage the U.S. to prepare itself for war and to look at developing its military. To him, this preparedness was important, as he could foresee the U.S. being dragged into what was going on over the Atlantic.

Roosevelt felt strongly that the United States should not sit back and wait until things got worse. Instead, he believed that they had to take action now and join the war effort in an attempt to stop things from spiraling out of control. He was disappointed when he discovered that President Wilson was of the opinion that the United States should remain neutral and that there was no need for them to improve their military.

This did of course change in 1917 when the U.S. was eventually dragged in. Even at this point, Roosevelt felt the need to get involved. He made clear his plans to create a volunteer division in order to help the war effort, but these plans were rejected, even though all four of his sons would go on to volunteer and cross the Atlantic to take part in the fighting. This would ultimately end in tragedy for Roosevelt, as one of his sons was shot down and killed, an event that then sent him into a depression.

That was not to say that he completely changed his mind about war, but he appeared to lose some of his enthusiasm, and people noted that the way in which he spoke about war was not as vigorous as before. However, it did not stop him from touring the country in order to give speeches in support of American involvement.

Chapter 9: Issues with His Presidency

Even though he was lauded by the people for the majority of the time that he was president, it is also fair for us to state that Roosevelt was not always regarded as being correct with everything that he attempted to do.

It is easy for us to identify specific issues with his presidency, but the truth of the matter is that the main problem was directly linked to the way in which he quite openly tackled those that had previously believed themselves to be above the command of the president. His main issue was undoubtedly corruption, which had reached endemic levels and had worked its way through so many aspects of society that it was difficult to distinguish between those that were not caught up in it with those that were corrupt to the core.

The problem for Roosevelt with his presidency was that the problems he wished to tackle were often too big for him to completely clear up, even after he was able to circumvent restrictions on his powers and avoid running into conflicts with Congress. The problems that he had wanted to resolve were too ingrained in the fabric of society. Often it was merely a case of him having to find some kind of common ground, whereby he could move things along even just slightly to save face on all sides.

In addition, there were a number of areas where he simply was unable to make the changes that he so wished. He made the wrong kind of impact in the eyes of his opponents when he invited Booker T. Washington to the White House, but at the same time it did show him just how bad the race issue was across the country.

Considering the relative success of his policies both domestically as well as internationally, it is difficult for us to come to any real conclusion as to there being major problems with his presidency. Some may argue that he did not do enough to combat corruption or the power that was held by various businesses, but he himself put that complaint to bed by comparing it to them turning the country back decades rather than looking towards prosperity.

If anything, we could state that the main issue with his presidency was the constant battle against those in Washington that always sought to undermine his power and to defeat his ideas. Due to the way in which he was often similar to a maverick figure, he had to fight a lone battle, with even those in the Republican Party being reluctant to accept as many changes as he would have liked to have made.

Chapter 10: Leading Up to His Death

Theodore Roosevelt was still extremely active in the last few years of his life. As we previously stated, he was desperate to become involved in aspects of World War I, even though that could potentially be linked to his absolute distrust of the German Kaiser, and even after this he was still involved in politics, albeit in a much quieter way than he had previously been used to.

We discussed aspects of his later life in our chapter on the things he became involved in after his time as President, but it is important to mention how those events could really be seen as triggering the eventual downfall, and death, of a once popular individual.

For most of his life he had looked to create history and change its course, but after 1912 he spent the majority of his time defending history and responding to events. He did remain in the public eye to a certain extent, as he was still popular in the media, but he did become increasing irrelevant, which was something that would have undoubtedly been upsetting to him.

He had been troubled by the stories that had began to emerge in the lead up to the 1912 election whereby he was accused of being a drunk, and this was something that would remain with him for the rest of his life. However, they had no basis for the accusations and he rightfully put it down to slander for election purposes.

After returning to New York from Brazil in 1914 he took the next couple of years to recover from his various exploits. However, he would find it difficult to remain out of the public eye for any real period of time, as can be seen by his reaction to the sinking of the Lusitania in 1915 where over 100 Americans were killed after the ship was sunk by a German U-Boat. Up until that point, he had largely kept quiet about the way in which Wilson was attempting to make sure that the United States remained neutral in World War 1. After this sinking, the general public of the United States did begin to change their mind as to whether or not the U.S. should get involved, and Roosevelt was at the forefront of that particular case of saber rattling.

Considering he was once the president, it is rather startling to see his reaction when the United States was eventually forced into the war, after Germany began dictating how and when ships could reach their shores. Upon the announcement that they were joining the war alongside the British, it is known that Roosevelt immediately made his way to Washington, barely able to hide his delight and enthusiasm at the drama that was unfolding before him. He went to Washington to ask permission to create his own band of warriors, in much the same way he had been allowed to do in the Spanish-American war some years earlier. It was perhaps for the best that this particular request was rejected by President Wilson.

By the time we get to the end of the war in 1918, we see a different side to Roosevelt, one that is barely recognizable as the energetic individual that had become all too familiar over the previous few decades. The death of his son in the war had affected him badly, but by this point it was his physical health that was eventually letting him down. Indeed, as the world was celebrating the end of the war, Theodore Roosevelt was busy having an operation to drain an abscess in his leg that had once again flared up. In addition, he was also suffering from rheumatism and was confined to his bed for several months towards the end of the year. In actual fact, upon admittance to hospital in New York, he was informed that there was a real risk that he would be confined to a wheelchair for the rest of his life.

This is not to say that he had retired from working in some kind of public capacity. Even though his health was not quite as it once was, he would spend his days writing various editorials for a number of newspapers. He was asked to once again become involved in politics, and some people even suggested that he would run for the role of president in 1920, but he made it clear that he had no desire to do so.

Even if he had, it would not have worked out, as Theodore Roosevelt died on January 5, 1919, at his home on Long Island. He died peacefully and suddenly due to a blood clot in his coronary artery. His death marked the end of one of the best presidents that the country had ever been lucky enough to have.

Chapter 11: His Legacy

When looking at the legacy of Theodore Roosevelt, it becomes clear that he is viewed in a positive manner, even close to 100 years after his death. He is viewed by many as being the first really modern President of the United States and indeed a number of scholars that focus on the issue of the Presidency will state that the amount of influence it has on daily life is all thanks to changes that Roosevelt implemented.

It is important to remember that in the 1800's it was Congress that was regarded as being the most powerful aspect of government. The president was then seen as being a figurehead in some respects. This was something that began to change in the 1880's.

It was Roosevelt who was responsible for making the president the most influential part of U.S. politics, taking over from Congress or even the political parties that had previously dominated proceedings. Implementing these changes required an individual that was not only confident in their own ability, but also confident that they had the support of the people, as he would have known that there would be some resistance within Congress itself.

An important part of his legacy should also be the way he put the rights of the people before anything else. In his eyes, being president meant that he had a unique relationship with the citizens of the United States, and he had to understand that there was a sense of responsibility to them as well.

Theodore Roosevelt took the concept of the president and changed it forever. He gave the president the power to be able to tackle those individuals and businesses that believed they were bigger than the law, and he also showed the ability to look past the Senate and Congress regarding reforms.

Presidents Since Roosevelt

We do not mean to look at each person that has since become president, but in order to determine his legacy it is useful to summarize how he has been viewed by those that followed.

He is rightfully viewed as the president that turned the role into one of a celebrity, and that is something that each president since Roosevelt has been only too happy to continue. In addition, his policies and the methods by which he installed change have largely been continued by those that have come after him, with a number of individuals openly referring to him on a number of occasions.

Presidents since Roosevelt understandably see him as an individual to look up to, no matter if they are a Democrat or a Republican. He is admired for the strength of his convictions and having the confidence to use his executive orders when he believed that what he was doing was genuinely for the good of the country. His willingness to then potentially fall on his sword should he be wrong is also to be admired, although this was not something that he then had to actually do.

So, how can we conclude the discussion about his legacy? Perhaps the best way is by looking at how the United States changed under his charge. He took the country from being a relatively weak country to one that was dominating not only North America but the world in general. The nation also changed from being quite conservative to being progressive, not only in its economy, but also in the way that it thought. Before Roosevelt, the United States had set on a path of destroying Mother Nature. It became a country that was intent on trying to preserve as much as possible through national parks.

He protected, developed, and grew the country and brought it to brand new heights that had never been reached before. He took the country out of the nineteenth century and effectively slammed it into the twentieth century, setting it up for a decade of dominance. His legacy is undoubtedly the way in which the United States was not only viewed at the time of his presidency, but has continued to be viewed ever since.

However, perhaps the best legacy that he has given the country is the national parks as we have discussed before. Those vast green spaces that have become such a focal point of life in the United States would simply not have existed had it not been for his foresight to change the way in which the country was using its natural resources. Now, millions of people each year can enjoy what he has left behind for future generations. The country itself would have undoubtedly looked completely different had it not been for his determination that large swathes of the country be protected in this way.

His legacy is secured purely on that basis alone.

Chapter 12: The Overall Conclusion of Theodore Roosevelt

So, what can we conclude about the life of Theodore Roosevelt? Perhaps we should begin this summary by stating that even though this was an individual that was born into an affluent family, he did not allow this to guide his way through life. He was determined to stick to his word even if those words or ideas went against the grain of pretty much every other individual that he encountered. He simply did not care whose toes he stepped on to get what he wanted. This was not due to a narcissistic point of view. He was an individual that weighed up the options before pushing forward in the direction that he deemed to be best.

This was a man who was very strong willed, not caring about who he upset in order to get his point across. At the same time, he was also not afraid to tackle those that deemed themselves to be bigger than the establishment, a personal quality that set him out as being completely different to those that had gone before him.

We have to conclude that his approach to politics, mixed in with his ability to leave certain influential individuals irate with his approach, helped him in ways that even he could not have imagined. The idea of him becoming president may not have even happened had he not become a thorn in the side of a Senator who then sought to get him nominated for the vice-president just to remove him from his direct line of fire.

Theodore Roosevelt was a man that was used to overcoming odds. He was able to do things without the overall stress of having to earn money just to survive. He battled against childhood illness, which at that point in history could have easily been fatal, in order to become not only extremely fit, but grow in stature as a human being.

This was an individual that would quite happily go against the grain if he believed that this was the correct direction in which to go. He could have so easily slipped into the background of society and lived quietly, but this was a man for which being quiet was never an option. He could have opted for an easier life as a lawyer and made a substantial sum of money in the process, but as had been pointed out repeatedly, money was not something that was of interest to him and this undoubtedly shaped his entire approach to life.

Roosevelt turned so many aspects of American culture and society on its head. He tackled problems from a moral perspective and was never afraid to shake things up if he believed it was for the greater good. He fought against corruption. He fought against companies trying to create a monopoly on the economy. He fought for a fair deal for everybody. He fought for improved conditions for workers. He saw injustices on various levels and came to the conclusion that things had to change.

His attacks on corruption are something to be admired, considering how it was built into the very fabric of society at that time. He had to tackle the biggest people in the country, but was never afraid to do so. He broke up companies that felt they were above such actions and forced them into providing better conditions for their workers, which was something completely new. When you look at the way in which he sought to make comprehensive changes in the law, the way Congress was run, and bring companies and individuals to task for their actions, you can begin to really understand why the business world was so against him getting into the White House.

It is no surprise that Theodore Roosevelt was a man that was not only admired, but a man that changed the concept of what the presidency was all about. All of those that have since followed him may have had their own unique way of tackling a variety of issues, but it is no coincidence that they feel the need to refer to "Teddy" and to look at his way of running the country as their inspiration.

He showed what was possible as long as you had the conviction within yourself to make the changes that were necessary. He took the United States and modernized it and made it a fairer market in line with his own ideals and those of so many that lived in the country at the time.

He strengthened its position in the world and created the role for which it is now famous: being the police force of the world and the country that is the main deal broker for issues that not only affect the world in general. He brokered treaties; he even pushed forward the idea of the Panama Canal. He built an international reputation as an individual that other world leaders would confer with. He was respected as being a wise individual who was able to weigh up the different options before taking any action.

Both the United States and the world in general have a lot to be grateful for when it comes to Theodore Roosevelt, because who knows what the global economy would have been like, with huge conglomerations controlling every aspect of our lives, if it was not for this forward thinker that was willing to tackle those that thought they were untouchable.

Theodore Roosevelt was an outstanding individual and an outstanding President.

References and Resources
Theodore Roosevelt: The President that Changed America

Edmund Morris: The Rise of Theodore Roosevelt

Tom Lansford: Theodore Roosevelt in Perspective

Sean Andrews: 101 Things Everybody Should Know About Theodore Roosevelt

Arthur G. Sharp: The Everything Theodore Roosevelt Book

Robert Green: Theodore Roosevelt

Dan Elish: Theodore Roosevelt

Edward Ayers: American Passages: A History of the United States

The Miller Center: Theodore Roosevelt Essays

http://www.britannica.com/biography/Edith-Roosevelt

http://www.sheppardsoftware.com/History/presidents/Presidents_26_Roosevelt.htm

http://www.pbs.org/wgbh/americanexperience/features/general-article/tr-early/

http://www.pbs.org/wgbh/americanexperience/features/general-article/tr-legacy/

http://www.sparknotes.com/biography/troosevelt

http://www.history.com/topics/us-presidents/theodore-roosevelt

http://www.biography.com/people/theodore-roosevelt-9463424

http://www.nps.gov/thri/theodorerooseveltbio.htm

http://www.thecrimson.com/article/1957/12/12/theodore-roosevelt-at-harvard-pthe-crimson/

http://www.nobelprize.org/nobel_prizes/peace/laureates/1906/roosevelt-bio.html

http://www.theodorerooseveltcenter.org/

Made in the USA
Middletown, DE
11 February 2016